The QUINOA QUOOKBOOK

Other books by Eliza Cross

101 Things To Do With Bacon

The Rusty Parrot Cookbook

Family Home of the New West

Food Lovers' Guide to Colorado

The QUINOA QUOOKBOOK

**100 Quintessential Recipes
Featuring Quinoa—
the "Super Food"**

By Eliza Cross

Drawings by Betty Crosslen

First Edition
10 9 8 7 6 5 4 3 2 1

Drawings by Betty Crosslen
Cover images licensed from Fotolia

Published by
Providence Publishers
www.providencepublishers.com

ISBN 10: 0615898521
ISBN 13: 978-0615898520

For Debbie
"Mother Smythe"
Christopher

Chenopodium quinoa

CONTENTS

INTRODUCTION

The first time I ordered quinoa from a menu, I pronounced it the way it looked to me: "kee-*noah.*" The waiter furrowed his furry eyebrows until my fellow diner whispered, "It's actually pronounced '*keen*-wah.'" Say wah?

The little grain with the funny name isn't technically a grain, but the seed of a vegetable similar to spinach and Swiss Chard. Quinoa's fan club has been going strong for 5,000 years; the ancient South American Incas reportedly called quinoa "the mother of all grains," which I think they meant as a compliment. Long before energy drinks or Viagra had been invented, Inca warriors ate quinoa to increase their stamina before battles and other manly pursuits.

A "Super Food"

Like most seeds—which contain within their tiny hulls the miraculous makings of a full-sized plant—quinoa is a very nutritious little bundle of nutty goodness. It has the special distinction of being the *only* vegetable that's a complete protein, which means that quinoa alone contains all nine of the essential amino acids necessary to meet the dietary needs of humans.

These amino acids play a key role in our health, from helping our bodies repair tissue to building new cells—which is comforting if you drank Long Island Iced Teas or "Mind Eraser" shots in your twenties.

Quinoa has a low glycemic index, which means it won't raise your blood sugar like, say, custard-filled maple Long Johns or deep-fried macaroni and cheese on a stick. Quinoa is gluten-free and rich in antioxidants and minerals like calcium, iron and magnesium. It contains more protein than any other grain—an average of 16.2 percent. You can see why quinoa has been dubbed the "super food."

It's true that quinoa is an especially good choice for vegans, vegetarians, those who can't tolerate gluten, and people who want to eat healthier. Perhaps because it has all those nutritional qualities for people on special diets, quinoa often seems to be relegated to vegan, gluten-free and 'lite' recipes. It's a wonderful addition to those diets, of course, but quinoa offers so much more.

A Culinary Superstar

With its nutty taste, fine texture and that delightful little burst you get when you bite down on it, quinoa deserves to shine in its own right. Some of the recipes in these pages are naturally low in fat or calories, but that's not this cookbook's primary focus. Instead, these quintessential recipes celebrate quinoa's delicious taste and texture, and pair it with a wide range of complimentary ingredients and flavors.

Many of these recipes will appeal to "flexitarians"—those of us who mostly eat healthfully, but occasionally succumb to a hearty slab of barbecued ribs or a few slices of crispy, crunchy bacon. In fact, now would probably be a good time to mention that this book features a recipe for Quinoa "Fried Rice," which includes *both* pork and bacon. The dish is one of my family's favorite dinners, and I think you'll love the way the quinoa complements the crispy bacon, tender snow peas and flavorful pork.

You'll also find healthy salads, soul-soothing soups, hearty breakfasts and dinners, mouth-watering appetizers, easy side dishes and decadent desserts in this recipe collection. Once you start cooking with quinoa, you may be inspired to use it in many everyday dishes.

Final Word

I recently heard quinoa described as "a good substitute for rice or barley." Blarney! Quinoa is too delicious and nutritious to play second fiddle to those plain grains. We've never been big barley eaters, but our family now prefers quinoa over rice in just about everything. Quinoa is delicious on its own, too; sometimes we make a simple dish of quinoa topped with a little butter, Parmesan cheese, salt and pepper...ahh, pure comfort food.

Whether you're already keen on quinoa or just now learning how to pronounce it, I hope you'll enjoy this collection of quintessential, easy-to-prepare recipes.

~Eliza Cross

COOKING TIPS

Colorful Quinoa

If you happen to live high up in the Andes Mountains, you'll be psyched to know that the *Chenopodium* quinoa plant will probably flourish in your hot, dry back yard. Also, if your neighbor has an unsightly RV camper or a rusted-out above-ground swimming pool, you'll have more reasons to celebrate because quinoa stalks can grow as tall as nine feet tall. Can you say "edible privacy fence"?

More than 120 varieties of quinoa varieties have been identified, but you'll generally find quinoa grouped in one of these three color categories:

White or ivory quinoa is the most common variety. It has a mild, nutty flavor and is extremely versatile.

Red quinoa is a good choice for meat dishes, and is also perfect for cold salads because it holds its shape well after cooking.

Exotic **black quinoa** tastes slightly sweeter, and retains its black color after cooking.

I've suggested a particular quinoa type in a few of the recipes, but generally you can simply choose whichever quinoa color you like best. Some markets sell a rainbow blend of all three colors if you want to be extra-groovy.

6 Steps to Perfect Quinoa

Quinoa is extremely easy to cook, and because it's not starchy it doesn't require lots of picky timing. But before you cook it, you do need to give it a good, brisk washing.

Step 1 (the MOST IMPORTANT step): Rinse and repeat.

I recently had a quinoa salad at a potluck that tasted faintly bitter. I knew right away that the quinoa hadn't been thoroughly washed. The **most crucial secret** to really tasty quinoa is to rinse it really, really well before cooking.

Mother Nature gave quinoa a natural coating that protects the grains, a soap-like substance called saponin. To remove the saponin, pour the uncooked quinoa in a bowl, add water and swish it around with your hands to remove the coating.

Now, dump the quinoa in a strainer and rinse it again under running water to get off every last bit of the coating. This will make all the difference and remove any traces of bitterness. Your quinoa will be slightly sweet and nutty—sort of like this author on a good day.

Step 2: Add liquid and bring to a boil.

You can cook your quinoa in many liquids. Water is commonly used, but stock and broth will impart quinoa with a nice flavor. In this book, I generally recommend 2 parts liquid to 1 part quinoa, but you may need more or less liquid depending on your climate, altitude and the moisture content of your quinoa.

Unlike rice, quinoa won't get mushy, stick together or throw a hissy fit if you add a little liquid if it's too dry, or cook off a little extra liquid. So relax, and simply combine your quinoa, liquid of choice and salt (if using) in a saucepan. Bring it to a boil over medium-high heat.

Step 3: Cover and cook.

Reduce the heat to simmering and cover the pot with a lid. Let it cook for about 15 minutes without peeking or stirring.

Step 4: Sample time.

Remove the lid, taste a bite of the quinoa to see if it's tender, and put the lid back on the pan. If the quinoa's texture is chewy you may wish to cook it for a few more minutes.

Step 5: Just walk away.

Once it's cooked to your liking, remove the pan from the heat and let it sit, covered, for another 5 to 10 minutes.

Step 6: Fluff time.

Use a fork to gently separate and "fluff" the grains. Serve and enjoy.

Optional Step: Toast Your Quinoa

Toasting the quinoa before cooking gives it a light brown color and enhances its naturally nutty flavor. After following Step #1 and giving the quinoa a thorough washing, spread the rinsed, drained quinoa in a nonstick skillet and cook over medium high heat, stirring frequently, for five minutes, or until quinoa just begins to turn pale brown. Remove from the heat, add the toasted quinoa to the liquid and continue with Step #2.

Storing Quinoa

To preserve its nutrients, I like to store **uncooked quinoa** in an airtight container in the refrigerator and use it within six months. It will likely last much longer, (some doomsday preppers give quinoa an eight-year refrigerated shelf life) but a fresh product will give you the tastiest results.

Cooked quinoa can be stored, tightly covered, in the refrigerator for two days.

FAQQs

Q: What does 'FAQQs' stand for?
A: Frequently asked quinoa questions.

Q: How much cooked quinoa does dry quinoa yield?
A: 1 cup of dry quinoa usually cooks up to about 2 1/2 to 3 cups of cooked quinoa.

Q: How much liquid do I need to cook quinoa?
A: To cook 1 cup of quinoa, you need about 2 cups liquid. You may need more or less depending on the type of quinoa.

Q: How long does it take to cook quinoa?
A: 1 cup of quinoa will usually cook in about 15 to 20 minutes. Your results may vary.

Q: How do I make quinoa less bitter?
A: The natural bitterness of quinoa's outer saponin coating can be removed by a vigorous swishing with water followed by another good rinsing in a fine mesh strainer.

Q: How do I make better-tasting quinoa?
A: You can enhance the flavor by adding 1/4 to 1/2 teaspoon of salt to each cup of dry quinoa and cooking it in broth or stock. You can add aromatics like fresh thyme, a smashed whole garlic clove or a good grinding of black pepper.

Q: Can I use my rice cooker to make quinoa?
A: Yes! Just use the 2:1 liquid to quinoa ratio and follow the instructions on your rice cooker.

Recipe Guidelines

- The recipes in this book were tested using salted butter. If your butter is unsalted, no problem. You can just add a little extra salt if you like. Or not.
- 'Olive oil' means extra virgin olive oil.
- The word 'cinnamon' refers to ground cinnamon, and my favorite type is genuine Vietnamese cinnamon.
- When eggs are called for, I always mean large eggs. If your eggs are a different size, you can always add or subtract a little egg white.
- Flour is the regular, all-purpose variety. I usually use organic, white whole wheat flour or a combination of unbleached white and whole wheat flour.
- Baking powder is double-acting baking powder. I'm a fan of non-GMO, aluminum-free Rumford brand.
- Honey can be raw or cooked, filtered or unfiltered, and preferably local.
- I usually cook with fine-grain sea salt, but table salt is fine in these recipes, too.
- Sugar is granulated, and if possible, choose organic cane sugar.
- 'Vanilla' refers to vanilla extract.
- Most of these recipes are not highly seasoned to allow for individual preferences, so you may wish to add additional salt and pepper.

Knife Terms

Chopped – roughly cut in 1/2-inch or smaller pieces.

Diced – chopped in tiny cubes, 1/4- to 1/3-inch in size.

Finely chopped – roughly cut in 1/4- to 1/3-inch pieces.

Julienned – cut in long, skinny strips.

Minced – cut in very small pieces, 1/8-inch or smaller.

BREAKFASTS & BREADS

Banana Maple Quinoa Pancakes

These tender flapjacks combine several favorite breakfast ingredients—quinoa, vanilla Greek yogurt, bananas and maple syrup.

1 cup cooked quinoa
3/4 cup flour
1/2 teaspoon cinnamon
1 1/2 teaspoons baking powder
1/4 teaspoon salt
2 large very ripe bananas, pureed
2 egg yolks
1/3 cup vanilla Greek yogurt
2 tablespoons milk
2 tablespoons maple syrup
1 tablespoon light or dark brown sugar
1 teaspoon vanilla
2 stiffly beaten egg whites
1/2 tablespoon butter

In a large bowl, whisk together the quinoa, flour, cinnamon, baking powder and salt. In a medium bowl, whisk together the bananas, egg yolks, yogurt, milk, maple syrup, brown sugar and vanilla until smooth. Add the egg mixture to the flour mixture, and whisk to combine. Fold the egg whites into the mixture just until combined.

Melt the butter in a nonstick griddle over medium heat. Pour 1/4 cup batter for each pancake onto hot griddle. Cook until bubbles appear on top, about 2 minutes. Flip and cook until golden brown on underside, about 2 minutes. Repeat with remaining batter. 4 servings.

Quinoa Hash Browns

Quinoa replaces the potatoes in these crispy, golden hash browns.

1 1/2 teaspoons extra virgin olive oil
1 small onion, finely chopped
3 cups cooked white quinoa
1 egg, beaten
1/2 teaspoon salt
1/2 teaspoon freshly ground black pepper
1 tablespoon butter

Heat the olive oil in a skillet over medium heat and cook the onions, stirring occasionally, until they are translucent and starting to brown around the edges. Use a slotted spoon to transfer the onions to a medium bowl, and don't wipe out the oil that remains in the skillet.

Add the cooked quinoa, beaten egg, salt and pepper to the onions in the bowl, and stir until combined. Heat the butter with the reserved oil in the skillet. Using a large spoon, drop generous spoonfuls of the quinoa mixture into the hot skillet. Flatten slightly with a spatula and cook for several minutes or until golden and crisp. Flip and cook until the other side is crispy and golden brown. Remove from the pan and repeat with the remaining batter. 4 to 6 servings.

Spinach, Egg and Quinoa Scramble

Start your day with a well-balanced breakfast with this easy, one-pan scramble.

8 eggs
1/4 cup milk
1 tablespoon butter
1 1/2 cups cooked quinoa
2 cups baby spinach leaves
salt and freshly ground black pepper to taste
1/3 cup shredded Colby-Jack cheese

Whisk the eggs and milk together in a bowl until combined. Melt the butter over medium heat in a large skillet. Pour in the egg mixture and begin to gently scramble the eggs, using a spatula to move the mixture to one side of the pan. Add the quinoa to the other side of the pan, and add the spinach to the middle of the pan. Continue cooking until the spinach wilts and the eggs are cooked. Gently stir to combine and season with salt and pepper. Sprinkle the cheese on top and serve. 4 servings.

Quinoa Quiche

Mushrooms, spinach and red bell pepper blend with quinoa for a colorful, flavorful breakfast quiche that's perfect for brunch.

1 tablespoon olive oil
1 small shallot, minced
half a red bell pepper, finely diced
1/4 pound button mushrooms, sliced
1 cup baby spinach leaves
1/4 teaspoon salt
1/4 teaspoon freshly ground black pepper
5 eggs
1/2 cup cooked quinoa
1/4 cup freshly grated Parmesan cheese
1 9-inch uncooked pie crust, fitted into a glass
    pie pan

Preheat oven to 350 degrees F. Heat the oil in a skillet over medium high, add the shallot and cook for one minute. Add the red bell pepper and mushrooms and continue cooking until the peppers are tender and the mushrooms begin to brown, about five minutes. Add the spinach, salt and pepper and cook until spinach is wilted, about one minute. Remove from heat and cool for five minutes.

In a large bowl, whisk the eggs until frothy. Add the spinach mixture, cooked quinoa and Parmesan cheese, and whisk just until combined. Pour the mixture into the prepared pie crust and bake for 40 minutes or until set in the middle. Let rest 10 minutes, slice and serve. 6 servings.

Healthy Quinoa Breakfast Skillet

Tender kale is paired with quinoa, eggs, fresh avocado and tomato in this easy Mexican scramble.

1 tablespoon butter
1 tablespoon olive oil, plus extra for cooking
1 bunch kale, washed and thinly sliced
2 cups just-cooked quinoa
half a lime
1 tablespoon chopped fresh cilantro
1 tomato, diced
1 avocado, peeled and diced
4 eggs
salt and freshly ground black pepper to taste
salsa or hot sauce

Heat the butter and olive oil in a skillet over medium heat until the butter melts. Add the kale and cook, stirring occasionally, until the kale is tender. Remove from heat. Add the quinoa and stir with a fork to fluff and combine. Squeeze the lime over the top and add the chopped cilantro. Add the chopped tomatoes and avocado, gently folding it into the quinoa mixture just until combined. Cover and set aside.

Lightly brush a skillet with olive oil and crack the eggs into the pan. Cook the eggs over medium heat until they are set and cooked to your liking. Season with salt and pepper. To serve, divide the quinoa mixture among four plates and top with a fried egg and a spoonful of salsa or a dash of hot pepper sauce. 4 servings.

Southwestern Quinoa Breakfast Wraps

A breakfast burrito is a great choice when you're on the run, and this recipe pairs quinoa with scrambled eggs and fresh veggies for a hearty start to the day.

1 tablespoon butter
2 green onions, finely chopped
6 eggs, lightly beaten
1/2 cup cooked quinoa
1/4 teaspoon salt
1/4 teaspoon freshly ground black pepper
6 8-inch flour tortillas, warmed
2 tablespoons sour cream
1/2 cup shredded Cheddar cheese
1/2 cup shredded lettuce
1 avocado, peeled and diced
1/2 cup fresh pico de gallo or salsa

Melt the butter in a large skillet over medium heat. Add the green onions and cook for one minute. Add the eggs and cook, stirring occasionally, until the eggs are softly cooked. Add the quinoa and stir gently just to combine; season with salt and pepper.

Spread each of the 6 tortillas with about 1 teaspoon sour cream. Spoon the egg mixture into the tortillas, dividing evenly. Top with cheese, lettuce and avocado. Roll up the burritos and spoon some of the pico de gallo or salsa on top. 6 wraps.

Golden Quinoa Florentine Benedict

Perfect for brunch, golden brown quinoa patties are topped with seasoned spinach, Canadian bacon and creamy Hollandaise Sauce.

For the Hollandaise Sauce:
3 large egg yolks, slightly beaten
2 teaspoons fresh lemon juice
dash of salt
dash of white pepper
dash of cayenne pepper
3/4 cup (1 1/2 sticks) butter

For the Quinoa Florentine:
2 teaspoons olive oil, divided
6 thick slices Canadian bacon
1 1/2 cups cooked quinoa
2 large eggs, lightly beaten
1/4 teaspoon salt
1/2 teaspoon freshly ground black pepper
3 tablespoons finely chopped fresh chives
1/4 cup finely chopped onion
1/4 cup grated Mozzarella cheese
1 clove garlic, finely chopped
1/2 cup bread crumbs, plus more if needed
1 pound fresh baby spinach leaves
additional salt and pepper to taste
paprika for garnish

Preheat the oven to 200 degrees F. To make the sauce, combine the egg yolks, lemon juice, salt, white pepper and cayenne pepper in a food processor or blender and blend thoroughly for one minute, until thick and creamy. Melt the butter in a small saucepan over medium heat.

Turn the food processor or blender on, and slowly pour in the hot butter. Blend until thickened, about 30 seconds. Cover and keep warm.

Brush a large skillet with 1 teaspoon olive oil and heat on medium-high. Cook the Canadian bacon slices on both sides until lightly browned. Transfer to an ovenproof dish or plate, cover with a lid or foil and keep warm in the oven.

Combine the quinoa, eggs, salt and pepper in a medium bowl. Stir in the chives, onion, cheese, and garlic. Add the bread crumbs, stir, and let sit for a few minutes so the crumbs can absorb some of the moisture. Shape the mixture into 6 round patties, about 1/2 inch thick. (If the mixture is too thin to shape easily, add more bread crumbs. If it seems too thick, add a little water.)

Heat the remaining 1 teaspoon olive oil in the same skillet over medium heat, add three of the quinoa patties, cover, and cook for about 7 minutes on each side, or until golden brown. Remove from the skillet and cool on an ovenproof plate while you cook the remaining patties. Keep patties warm in the oven and don't wipe out the skillet.

Add the spinach to the skillet and cook over medium heat, stirring frequently, until spinach is tender. Season with salt and pepper. To serve, arrange a quinoa patty on each of six warmed plates. Arrange a slice of Canadian bacon on each patty and top with the seasoned spinach. Pour a generous spoonful of Hollandaise Sauce over the spinach and sprinkle with paprika. 6 servings.

Blueberry Lemon Quinoa Crunch Muffins

These large, bakery-sized muffins are topped with a sweet, crunchy topping. Adding frozen blueberries at the last minute is the secret to keeping the berries whole while baking (and they won't turn your batter blue!)

For the topping:
1/2 cup sugar
1/3 cup flour
4 tablespoons cold butter, cut in small pieces
1 1/2 teaspoons cinnamon

For the muffins:
1 1/4 cups flour
1 1/2 teaspoons baking powder
1 teaspoon salt
1/4 teaspoon cinnamon
1 tablespoon grated lemon zest
3/4 cup sugar
1/4 cup vegetable oil
1 1/4 cups cooked quinoa
1/2 cup sour cream
3 tablespoons fresh lemon juice
1 egg
1 teaspoon vanilla
1 cup frozen blueberries (do not thaw)

To make the topping, combine the sugar, flour, butter and cinnamon in a small bowl. Combine with your fingers until butter is blended in and the mixture is crumbly; reserve.

Preheat the oven to 375 degrees F and grease a muffin pan or line it with paper liners. In a medium bowl, whisk together the flour, baking powder, salt and cinnamon. Stir the in lemon zest.

In a large bowl, whisk together the sugar and oil. Add the cooked quinoa, sour cream, lemon juice, egg and vanilla, stirring until fully blended. Stir the frozen blueberries into the flour mixture, and then fold the flour mixture into the quinoa mixture.

Spoon into the prepared muffin tin, about 2/3 full, and sprinkle with the topping. Bake for about 20 to 25 minutes, or until a toothpick inserted in the middle of a muffin comes out clean. 12 muffins.

Quinoa Carrot Cake Muffins

Like carrot cake for breakfast, these muffins combine red quinoa and carrots with raisins, applesauce and cinnamon. Your house will smell so good while they're baking!

1 cup flour
1 cup cooked red quinoa
2/3 cup sugar
2 teaspoons cinnamon
1/2 teaspoon nutmeg
2 teaspoons baking powder
1 cup sour cream
1/2 cup unsweetened applesauce
4 tablespoons honey
2 eggs
2 teaspoons vanilla
1 1/2 cup peeled and finely grated carrots
1/2 cup raisins

Preheat oven to 350 degrees F and grease a muffin tin or line with paper liners.

In a large bowl, whisk together the flour, quinoa, sugar, cinnamon, nutmeg, and baking powder. In a medium bowl, combine the sour cream, applesauce, honey, eggs and vanilla until smooth. Make a well in the flour mixture and pour in the applesauce mixture; stir just until combined (don't over-mix). Add the carrots and raisins, and stir until just combined. Spoon the batter into the prepared muffin tin, about 2/3 full. Bake for 18 to 22 minutes, or until a toothpick inserted in a muffin comes out clean. 12 muffins.

Quinoa Banana Pumpkin Bread

Bananas and pumpkins pair well with quinoa's nutty flavor in this easy-to-make quick bread.

1 1/2 cups whole wheat flour
3/4 cup brown sugar
1 teaspoon pumpkin pie spice
1 teaspoon baking powder
1/2 teaspoon baking soda
1/2 teaspoon salt
1 cup cooked quinoa
2 ripe bananas, peeled
2 eggs, lightly beaten
3/4 cup pumpkin puree
1/2 cup milk
4 tablespoons butter, melted
2 teaspoons vanilla

Preheat oven to 350 degrees F and grease a loaf pan.

In a large bowl, whisk together the flour, brown sugar, pumpkin pie spice, baking powder, baking soda and salt. Add the quinoa and whisk to mix evenly. In another bowl, mash the bananas with a fork. Add the eggs and pumpkin puree and stir until combined. Add the milk, melted butter and vanilla, and stir until combined.

Slowly add the pumpkin mixture to the quinoa mixture, and stir until just combined. Spoon the batter in the pan and smooth the top. Bake for 50-60 minutes, or until the top is golden brown and a toothpick comes out clean. 1 loaf.

Apple Maple Quinoa Granola

Why buy store-bought cereal when you can bake up a batch of this crispy, crunchy golden granola? It's lightly sweetened with maple syrup, honey and dried apples.

2 cups whole rolled oats
1/2 cup uncooked quinoa, rinsed and drained
1/2 cup dried apples, chopped
1/3 cup wheat germ
1/4 cup flax seed
1/2 cup raw shelled sunflower seeds
1/4 cup shredded coconut
2 teaspoons cinnamon
1/2 cup coconut oil
1/4 cup maple syrup
1/4 cup honey

Preheat the oven to 325 degrees F and line a large baking sheet with parchment paper. In a large bowl, combine the rolled oats, quinoa, dried apples, wheat germ, flax seed, sunflower seeds, coconut and cinnamon; mix well.

In a saucepan over medium heat, combine the coconut oil, maple syrup and honey and stir until the coconut oil melts and the mixture is combined. Drizzle over the oat mixture, stirring, until well combined. Spread on the prepared baking sheet and bake for 25 minutes. Remove from the oven and stir. Return to oven and cook for another 10 minutes, or until mixture is lightly browned and fragrant. Cool, crumble, and store in a tightly covered container. 8 servings.

Quinoa Waffles

Quinoa adds a tender, chewy bite to these crispy, golden waffles, sweetened with just a touch of maple syrup.

3/4 cup flour
1/2 cup rolled oats
2 teaspoons baking powder
1/2 teaspoon salt
1/4 teaspoons cinnamon
2 eggs
2 tablespoons melted butter
1/3 cup milk
2 tablespoons maple syrup
1 cup cooked quinoa

Lightly grease and preheat waffle iron.

In a medium bowl, whisk together the flour, rolled oats, baking powder, salt and cinnamon. In another bowl, whisk together the eggs, melted butter, milk and maple syrup until smooth. Add the egg mixture to the flour mixture and whisk to combine. Add the cooked quinoa and whisk to combine.

Ladle the batter into a preheated waffle iron. Cook the waffles until golden and crisp. Serve immediately. About 6 waffles.

Creamy-Crisp Quinoa Skillet Bread

Tender quinoa updates the flavor of this old-fashioned skillet bread, which has the surprise of a soft, creamy center. Serve it cut in wedges with butter and jam.

1 cup pastry flour
3/4 cup yellow cornmeal
1 teaspoon baking powder
1/2 teaspoon baking soda
2 eggs
1 1/2 cups cooked quinoa
3 tablespoons butter, melted
3 tablespoons brown sugar
3/4 teaspoon salt
2 cups milk
1 1/2 tablespoons white vinegar
1 cup heavy cream

Preheat the oven to 350 degrees F and place a rack in the upper third. Lightly grease a 10-inch cast-iron skillet. Put the skillet in the oven to preheat while you prepare the batter.

In a large bowl, whisk together the flour, cornmeal, baking powder and baking soda. In a separate bowl, beat the eggs, quinoa, and melted butter until blended. Add the brown sugar, salt, milk and vinegar and stir again. Add the quinoa mixture to the flour mixture and stir just until combined.

Remove the heated skillet from the oven and carefully spread the batter in it. Then pour the heavy cream all at once into the center of the batter. (Resist the temptation to stir the batter!)

Return to the oven and cook for 45 to 55 minutes, or until center is just set and top is lightly browned. Remove from the oven and cool. Cut in wedges and serve with butter and honey or jam. 8 servings.

Quinoa Corn Hush Puppies

Also known as "corn dodgers," these warm little morsels are sure to go quickly at your next gathering.

1 1/3 cups flour
2 teaspoons baking powder
3/4 teaspoon salt
1/2 teaspoon ground coriander
1/4 teaspoon paprika
1/4 teaspoon freshly ground black pepper
2 egg yolks
1/2 cup milk
1 1/2 cups cooked fresh or frozen corn, cooked
2/3 cup cooked quinoa
2 green onions, thinly sliced
2 egg whites, stiffly beaten
vegetable oil for frying (enough to reach a depth of
    2 inches in your sauté pan)

In a large mixing bowl, whisk together the flour, baking powder, salt, coriander, paprika and pepper. In a small bowl, combine the egg yolks and milk. Stir the egg mixture into the flour mixture until blended. Add the corn, quinoa and chopped green onions, and stir until combined. Gently fold in the egg whites.

Heat the cooking oil in a skillet over medium heat until it reaches 370 degrees F. Drop small spoonfuls of the batter in the hot oil and fry, turning once, until golden brown. Remove with a slotted spoon and drain on paper towels. Repeat with the remaining batter. 6 servings.

APPETIZERS

Cheesy Quinoa, Ham and Artichoke Bites

Mild artichokes and quinoa pair nicely with salty ham and sharp Cheddar cheese for a bite-sized appetizer full of flavor.

2 cups cooked quinoa
2 eggs
1 egg white
1 cup finely chopped canned, drained water-pack artichoke hearts
1 1/2 cups shredded sharp Cheddar cheese
1/2 cup diced ham
1/4 cup chopped parsley
2 tablespoons Parmesan cheese
2 green onions, finely sliced
1/2 teaspoon salt
1/4 teaspoon freshly ground black pepper

Preheat oven to 350 degrees F and grease a mini muffin tin. Combine all ingredients in a large bowl and stir gently until mixed. Spoon the mixture in the mini muffin tin, rounding the tops, and bake for 15 to 20 minutes, or until the edges are golden brown. Cool for 5 minutes before removing from the pan. Approximately 30 bites.

Quinoa-Parmesan Crisps

Lacy and delicate, these crisps are perfect with a glass of wine or as a garnish for a salad of lightly dressed field greens.

1/2 cup grated or shredded Parmesan cheese
1/4 cup cooked quinoa
1/8 teaspoon freshly ground black pepper

Preheat oven to 400 degrees F and combine the cheese, quinoa and pepper in a small bowl.

Spoon heaping tablespoons of the mixture onto a parchment- or silicone-lined baking sheet, spacing 1 inch apart, and lightly pat down to make a circle about 1/8 inch thick. Bake for 4 to 5 minutes or until golden and crisp.

Remove the pan from the oven, press down on the crisps with the underside of a thin metal spatula, and allow to cool in the pan. Remove from parchment or silicone with a spatula. 12 crisps.

Quinoa Lettuce Wraps

Crunchy lettuce wraps are the perfect first course for an Asian-themed dinner.

2 teaspoons sesame oil
2 tablespoons tamari or soy sauce
1 1/2 teaspoons water
1 tablespoon creamy peanut butter
1 1/2 teaspoons honey
1 tablespoon rice vinegar
2 teaspoons chili sauce
1 tablespoon butter
2 tablespoons minced onion
2 cloves garlic, peeled and minced
1-inch piece fresh ginger root, peeled and minced
1/2 teaspoon salt
1/4 teaspoon freshly ground black pepper
2 cups cooked quinoa
1/2 cup shelled, steamed edamame
1/4 cup chopped water chestnuts
1/4 cup finely chopped peanuts
12 lettuce leaves, rinsed and patted dry

In a small saucepan, combine the sesame oil, tamari or soy sauce, water, peanut butter, honey, rice vinegar and chili sauce. Cook over medium heat for two minutes, stirring, until mixture is smooth. Reserve.

Melt the butter in a large skillet over medium high heat. Add the onion, garlic, ginger, salt and pepper, and cook for five minutes, stirring occasionally.

Add the quinoa and reserved sauce to the skillet and stir to combine. Add the edamame and water chestnuts and continue cooking for about 2 minutes, until mixture is heated through. Sprinkle with chopped peanuts, and serve accompanied with lettuce leaves.

To eat, spoon some of the quinoa mixture down the center of a lettuce leaf and roll up like a burrito. 12 servings.

Quinoa Caviar

My prediction? You'll love this easy dip more than fish caviar. Black quinoa pairs well with the black beans, and you can serve this like salsa with tacos, quesadillas and enchiladas, too.

1/2 cup rice vinegar
1/4 cup sugar
1/4 cup extra virgin olive oil
1 teaspoon salt
1/2 teaspoon ground black pepper
2 cups cooked black quinoa
1 15 ounce can black beans, rinsed and drained
1 1/2 cups cooked fresh or frozen corn
1/2 cup diced celery
1/2 red bell pepper, diced
1/2 yellow bell pepper, diced
1 Anaheim pepper, finely diced
2 cloves garlic, peeled and finely minced
1/4 cup chopped cilantro
tortilla chips

In a saucepan over medium-high heat, combine the rice vinegar, sugar, olive oil, salt and pepper, and bring to a boil. Cook and stir until sugar is dissolved, about 5 minutes. Remove from heat and cool to room temperature.

In a large bowl, combine the quinoa, beans, corn, celery, peppers and garlic. Pour the dressing over the mixture, cover and refrigerate for 2 hours or overnight. Drain off any liquid, toss with the cilantro and serve accompanied with tortilla chips. 8 to 10 servings.

Buffalo Chicken Quinoa Bites

Enjoy the flavor of Buffalo chicken wings without the mess in these bite-sized appetizers that combine quinoa, chicken and spicy hot pepper sauce.

1 cup cooked quinoa
1 cup finely chopped cooked chicken
1/2 cup shredded mozzarella cheese
1/2 cup panko bread crumbs
1/4 cup minced onion
1/4 cup hot pepper sauce
1 egg, lightly beaten
1/2 teaspoon minced garlic
1/2 teaspoon salt
1/4 teaspoon freshly ground black pepper
1/2 cup prepared blue cheese dressing

Preheat the oven to 350 degrees F and grease a mini muffin tin.

In a medium bowl, combine the quinoa, chicken, mozzarella cheese, bread crumbs, minced onion, hot sauce, egg, garlic, salt and pepper, and stir just until combined.

Scoop one heaping tablespoon of the mixture into each well of the mini muffin tin, pressing down lightly to compact. Bake for 25 to 30 minutes. Cool and serve accompanied with blue cheese dressing for dipping. 24 bites.

Quinoa-Stuffed Cherry Tomatoes

Cute and colorful, these tiny hors d'oeuvres taste like a bite-sized BLT.

24 medium-sized cherry tomatoes (or more if tomatoes are small)
1/2 cup cooked quinoa
2 slices bacon, cooked, drained and finely crumbled
1/4 cup mayonnaise
1 finely minced green onion
2 tablespoons grated Parmesan cheese
1 tablespoon finely minced fresh parsley

Cut a thin slice off the top of each tomato. Use a grapefruit spoon or your fingers to scoop out the seeds and pulp. (These will not be used in the recipe.) Arrange the tomatoes cut-side down on a paper towel to drain.

In a small bowl, combine the quinoa, crumbled bacon, mayonnaise, green onion and Parmesan cheese. Spoon the mixture into the tomatoes and sprinkle with the parsley. Serve at once or chill for several hours. 24 pieces.

Crab, Corn and Quinoa Dip

The quinoa keeps this heavenly dip from tasting too rich—and be prepared, because everyone is going to ask you for the recipe.

1 tablespoon olive oil
1 shallot, peeled and minced
1 cup fresh corn kernels
2 garlic cloves, minced
1/2 teaspoon salt
1/4 teaspoon freshly ground black pepper
8 ounces lump crabmeat
1/2 cup cooked quinoa
1/4 cup cream cheese, softened
1/4 cup grated Monterey Jack cheese
1 teaspoon hot sauce
2 tablespoons finely chopped chives
2 tablespoons finely grated Parmesan cheese
crostini or crackers

Preheat the oven to 350 degrees F. Heat the oil in a sauté pan over medium heat and cook the shallot for two minutes. Add the corn and continue to cook for 3 minutes. Add the garlic, salt and pepper, and cook for another minute.

Spoon the corn mixture in a medium bowl and add the crab, quinoa, cream cheese, Monterey Jack cheese, hot sauce and chives. Stir gently to combine and spread the mixture in a one-quart baking dish. Sprinkle with the Parmesan cheese and bake for 20 to 25 minutes or until golden brown. Serve hot with crostini or crackers. 8 servings.

Quinoa Summer Rolls

Translucent rice paper wraps around a filling of seasoned quinoa and crunchy veggies for a cool appetizer that's as pretty as it is delicious.

1/2 teaspoon rice wine vinegar
1/2 teaspoon sesame oil
1 cup cooked quinoa
6 rice paper spring roll wrappers
6 leaves butter lettuce
12 large fresh mint leaves
1 large carrot, scraped or peeled and julienned
1/2 English cucumber, peeled and julienned
1 small red bell pepper, julienned
1/2 cup bean sprouts
salt and freshly ground black pepper to taste
soy sauce and sweet chili sauce for dipping

Combine the rice wine vinegar and sesame oil. In a small bowl, drizzle the mixture over the quinoa and reserve.

Fill a dish large enough to completely submerge the rice paper wrappers with an inch of warm water. Soak 1 rice paper wrapper for about 20 seconds or until soft. Lay the wrapper out on a cotton dish towel to absorb the excess water, and transfer it to a cutting board.

About a third of the way up from the bottom of the wrapper, tear one of the lettuce leaves and layer it in a 3-inch long row. Lay two of the mint leaves on top of the lettuce.

Spoon 2 tablespoons of the quinoa mixture in an even layer, followed by some of the carrots, cucumber, red bell pepper and bean sprouts. Season to taste with salt and pepper.

Fold the bottom of the rice paper wrapper over the vegetables, creating a tight roll. Turn in the sides and continue rolling up from the bottom. Repeat with remaining wrappers and ingredients. Slice each roll in half on the diagonal and serve with soy sauce and sweet chili sauce for dipping. 6 servings.

Crispy Quinoa Cups with Guacamole

They look complicated, but these little quinoa-cornmeal cups are easy to make and fill with a generous dollop of fresh guacamole. Arriba!

3/4 cup cooked quinoa
3/4 cup cornmeal
3/4 cup flour
1/2 teaspoon chili powder
1 shallot, finely chopped
1/2 teaspoon salt
1/4 teaspoon freshly ground black pepper
1/3 cup softened cream cheese
juice from 1 lime
water as needed
1 cup prepared guacamole
1 medium tomato, finely chopped

Preheat oven to 350 degrees F and lightly grease 24 mini muffin cups. In a large bowl, combine the cooked quinoa, cornmeal, flour, chili powder, shallot, salt and pepper. Cut the cream cheese in with a pastry cutter or knife and fork until well blended. Gradually add the lime juice and a few tablespoons of water until the mixture forms a workable dough. (Do not over-mix.)

Evenly distribute the batter into the muffins cups, gently pressing the dough up the sides to form a small shell. Bake for 20 minutes or until lightly browned. Cool for 5 minutes, remove cups from pan and finish cooling on a wire rack. Fill each cup with a heaping teaspoon of guacamole and garnish with chopped tomato. 24 pieces.

Crunchy Quinoa Chicken Fingers

Golden brown and cooked up fresh, these tasty chicken strips are a world away from the fast food variety. Kids love them, of course, but grown-ups do, too!

1 cup cooked quinoa
1 cup seasoned breadcrumbs
2 pounds boneless, skinless chicken breasts, cut
 in 1-inch long strips
1/2 teaspoon garlic powder
1/4 teaspoon salt
1/4 teaspoon freshly ground black pepper
1/4 teaspoon paprika
2 eggs
honey mustard sauce, ranch dressing, barbeque
 sauce or your favorite dipping sauce

Preheat the oven to 400 degrees F and grease a large cookie sheet. In a shallow bowl, combine the quinoa and breadcrumbs and mix together until blended; mixture will be dry. Sprinkle the chicken with garlic powder, salt, pepper and paprika. Beat the eggs in a shallow dish. Dip the chicken pieces in the egg and then into the quinoa mixture, patting to make the crumbs stick to the chicken.

Arrange on the baking sheet, and bake for 10 minutes. Remove from the oven, turn the tenders over, and continue baking for 10 more minutes, or until chicken is cooked through and tenders are lightly browned and crispy. Serve with dipping sauce on the side. 4 to 6 servings.

Quinoa Stuffed Mushrooms

A welcome update of the traditional recipe, this savory appetizer pairs red quinoa with tender mushrooms and Parmesan cheese.

24 large button mushrooms
2 tablespoons olive oil
2 cloves garlic, minced
1 1/2 cups cooked red quinoa
1/2 teaspoon salt
1/2 teaspoon freshly ground black pepper
1/4 cup grated Parmesan cheese, plus extra for
    topping
3 tablespoons finely chopped flat leaf parsley

Preheat the oven to 350 degrees F and grease a baking sheet. Wipe the mushrooms with a damp cloth and snap off the stems. Arrange the caps on the baking sheet. Finely chop the stems.

In a large skillet over a medium flame, heat the olive oil and add the chopped mushroom stems and garlic. Cook, stirring occasionally, for about 4 minutes, or until garlic starts to brown. Add the quinoa, salt and pepper, and continue to cook, stirring gently, for another 3 minutes. Remove from heat and add the Parmesan cheese and parsley, stirring just until combined.

Spoon the mixture into the mushroom caps and bake for 15 minutes, or until heated through and lightly browned. Remove from oven; transfer to a serving plate. Sprinkle with additional Parmesan cheese and serve warm. 24 pieces.

SOUPS, CHOWDERS & STEWS

Chicken and Quinoa Soup

If you think traditional chicken soup is comforting, wait until you try chicken soup enriched with nutritious quinoa. This soup is especially good when it's made with homemade stock.

1 tablespoon olive oil
1/2 onion, diced
6 carrots, thinly sliced
2 stalks celery, chopped
1 clove garlic, finely minced
1/3 cup uncooked quinoa, rinsed and drained
4 cups chicken stock or broth
1/2 pound boneless, skinless chicken, cut in thin
    strips
salt and freshly ground black pepper to taste

In a large pot set over medium-low heat, heat the olive oil and cook the onions, carrots and celery until tender, about 10 minutes. Stir in the garlic and quinoa, and cook for about a minute. Add the chicken stock, raise the heat to medium, and simmer for about 15 minutes. Add the chicken and simmer for 10 minutes, until the chicken is cooked through. Season with salt and pepper and serve. 4 servings.

Turkey Quinoa Tamale Soup

This rich, mildly spicy soup is a wonderful way to use leftover turkey after Thanksgiving, or you can substitute chicken for the turkey.

2 tablespoons olive oil
1 onion, chopped
3 stalks celery, diced
2 cups fresh corn kernels or thawed, frozen corn
1 teaspoon ground cumin
1/2 teaspoon dried oregano
1/4 teaspoon salt
1/4 teaspoon black pepper
2 tablespoon tomato paste
5 cups turkey or chicken stock or broth
2 cups chopped cooked turkey or chicken
1 cup cooked quinoa
2 1/2 cups broken corn tortilla chips, divided
1 cup shredded Monterey Jack cheese
1/4 cup chopped fresh cilantro leaves

In a large pot over medium-high flame, heat the olive oil and cook the onion for about 4 minutes, or just until translucent and tender. Add the celery and cook for 2 more minutes, stirring gently. Add the corn, cumin, oregano, salt, pepper and tomato paste and stir to blend.

Add the stock or broth, the turkey or chicken, the quinoa and 2 cups broken tortilla chips. Bring the soup to a boil, stirring occasionally. Reduce heat to low, cover, and simmer the soup for 30 minutes. Garnish with cheese, the remaining 1/2 cup chips and chopped cilantro. 6 servings.

Creamy Carrot Soup with Toasted Quinoa

This creamy soup combines the slightly-sweet flavor of fresh carrots with nutty, toasted quinoa.

3 tablespoons butter, divided
1 medium onion, diced
1 large clove garlic, peeled and minced
4 cups chicken stock
3 large carrots, peeled and shredded
1 tablespoon olive oil
1 1/2 cups cooked quinoa
1/2 cup heavy cream
salt and freshly ground black pepper to taste
chopped flat leaf parsley

In a heavy pot, melt 2 tablespoons butter over medium heat and sauté the onion and garlic until tender, stirring occasionally. Add the chicken stock and carrots, and simmer until the carrots are tender, about 15 minutes.

Meanwhile, heat the remaining 1 tablespoon butter and the olive oil in a large skillet over medium heat. Add the cooked quinoa and cook, stirring occasionally, until it is lightly browned, about 10 minutes. Remove from heat and reserve.

Working in batches, puree the soup in a blender or food processor until smooth. Return to the pot and add the cream. Stir and heat through, seasoning with salt and pepper. Divide the soup among 6 heated bowls and top with 1/4 cup toasted quinoa and chopped parsley. 6 servings.

White Quinoa Chili

A nice alternative to red chili, this creamy quinoa chili is always a big hit at potlucks.

1 pound dried navy beans
6 cups chicken stock
1/4 cup (half stick) butter
2 cloves garlic, minced
1 medium onion, diced
1 1/2 cups diced green chiles
1 cup uncooked white quinoa, rinsed and drained
1 tablespoon ground cumin
1 tablespoon dried oregano
1 teaspoon salt
1 teaspoon freshly ground black pepper
fresh lime wedges and sour cream

Rinse beans well, cover with cool water, and soak for 2 hours. Drain. Put the beans in large pot with the chicken stock and bring to a boil over high heat.

In a medium skillet, heat the butter over medium heat. Add the garlic, onion, and chiles and cook, stirring to prevent sticking, for 5 minutes. Add to the pot with beans, along with the quinoa, cumin, oregano, salt and pepper; stir to combine well.

Lower the heat to medium and cook, stirring occasionally, for about 1 1/2 hours or until the beans are tender. Serve with lime wedges and sour cream. 10 servings.

Cream of Tomato Soup with Crispy Quinoa

If you're accustomed to the red canned version, this creamy homemade soup with fresh tomatoes and nutty quinoa will rock your world!

1/2 teaspoon baking soda
5 large fresh tomatoes, chopped
6 tablespoons unsalted butter, divided
1 cup cooked quinoa
1 small onion, chopped
4 tablespoons flour
4 cups milk
1 teaspoon sugar
salt and ground white pepper to taste

In a small bowl, sprinkle the baking soda over the tomatoes and stir well. (This step reduces the acidity in the tomatoes and makes the flavor incredible!) Set aside.

In a large skillet, heat 1 tablespoon of the butter over medium heat. Add the cooked quinoa and cook, stirring occasionally, until it is lightly browned, about 10 minutes. Remove from heat and reserve.

In a large heavy saucepan, melt the remaining butter over medium heat. Add the onion and cook, stirring, until the onion is translucent. Sprinkle the flour over the mixture and cook, stirring for one minute. Slowly add the milk and sugar, and continue to cook, stirring, until thickened.

Add the tomatoes and bring just to a simmer. Remove from the heat and let sit for 5 minutes.

Strain the soup through a mesh strainer, pressing down on the solids to extract as much liquid as possible. Return the soup to the pot, season with salt and pepper, and cook just until heated through. Divide the soup among 6 heated bowls and garnish with a generous spoonful of toasted quinoa. 6 servings.

Italian Minestrone

Based on an old family recipe, this hearty soup has tons of fresh vegetables, beans, pasta and— surprise!—delicious quinoa.

1/4 pound bacon, diced
2 tablespoons butter
4 cloves garlic, peeled and minced
2 carrots, peeled and cut in 1/4-inch dice
1 onion, peeled and cut in 1/4-inch dice
1 leek (white part and about 1 inch of green part), well rinsed, quartered lengthwise and cut in 1/4-inch slices
3 cups finely shredded green cabbage
1/2 cup uncooked quinoa, rinsed and drained
1 small zucchini, quartered lengthwise and cut in 1/4-inch slices
1 potato, peeled and cut in 1/4-inch dice
4 cups chicken stock or broth
3 cups beef stock or broth
2 tablespoons tomato paste
5 tablespoons chopped fresh Italian flat-leaf parsley, divided (or substitute regular parsley)
2 teaspoons dried oregano
1-1/2 teaspoons dried basil
1 teaspoon salt
1/2 teaspoon freshly ground black pepper
1 15-ounce can cannellini beans, drained
4 ripe Roma tomatoes, cut in1/4-inch dice
freshly grated Parmesan cheese

Cook the bacon in a large heavy pot over low heat for about 8 minutes, until it barely starts to brown. Add the butter, and when it has melted add the garlic, carrots, onion and leek and raise the heat to medium. Cover and wilt the vegetables for 10 minutes, stirring occasionally.

Add the cabbage, quinoa, zucchini, potato, chicken stock, beef stock and tomato paste. Bring to a boil. Reduce the heat and add 2 tablespoons of the parsley, the oregano, basil, salt and pepper. Simmer over medium heat for 15 minutes.

Add the beans and tomatoes. Simmer for 10 minutes and adjust the seasonings. Stir in the remaining 3 tablespoons parsley just before serving, and garnish with Parmesan cheese. 6 to 8 servings.

Cream of Chicken and Quinoa Soup

This creamy chicken soup is thickened with an old-fashioned roux and is a great way to use leftover roasted chicken.

1/4 cup butter
3 large cloves garlic, peeled and minced
1 medium onion, chopped
1 medium carrot, peeled and shredded
6 stalks asparagus, finely diced
1/2 cup all-purpose flour
4 cups chicken stock, heated
1 cup cooked quinoa
1 cup finely chopped cooked chicken
1/2 teaspoon crumbled dried thyme
1 cup half and half
salt and freshly ground black pepper to taste
1 tablespoon chopped parsley

In a large saucepan, melt the butter over medium heat and sauté the garlic and onion until tender. Add the carrots and asparagus and cook several minutes, or until tender. Add the flour and cook over low heat for 5 minutes, stirring occasionally with a wooden spoon. Gradually add the hot chicken stock, stirring constantly until smooth. Add the quinoa, chopped chicken and thyme. Simmer for 15 minutes.

Add the half and half and salt and pepper; cook about 5 more minutes or until the soup is hot. Garnish with parsley and serve at once. 4 to 6 servings.

Autumn Cheddar Quinoa Soup

When the temperatures start to cool, this easy, cheesy soup is perfect for a weeknight dinner.

1 tablespoon extra-virgin olive oil
1/4 cup minced onion
2 stalks celery, chopped
2 medium carrots, peeled and cut in 1/2-inch dice
2 cloves garlic, minced
1 cup fresh or frozen, thawed cauliflower florets
1/2 cup uncooked quinoa, rinsed and drained
4 cups chicken broth
2 tablespoons flour
1 1/2 cups milk
1 cup grated extra sharp Cheddar cheese
salt and freshly ground black pepper to taste

Heat the olive oil in a heavy soup pot over medium-high heat, and sauté the onion for two minutes. Add the celery, carrots and garlic, and cook until the onion is translucent, about three more minutes. Add the cauliflower, quinoa and chicken broth and stir. Cover, reduce heat to medium-low and simmer for 20 minutes, or until vegetables are tender.

In a small bowl, combine the flour and milk and whisk together until smooth. Uncover the soup and slowly pour in the milk mixture, stirring constantly. Continue cooking and stirring until soup thickens. Slowly add the cheese and stir just until melted. Remove from heat, adjust seasonings and serve immediately. 6 servings.

Tuscan Tomato, Quinoa and White Bean Soup

With a satisfying blend of vegetables, beans, greens and quinoa, this rustic soup is especially good served with slices of warm ciabatta bread.

2 tablespoons olive oil
1 medium onion, diced
1 medium shallot, diced
2 stalks celery, diced
2 cloves garlic, peeled and minced
1 bay leaf
1/2 teaspoon finely chopped fresh thyme leaves
 or 1/4 teaspoon dried thyme
1/4 teaspoon finely chopped fresh rosemary or
1/8 teaspoon dried rosemary, leaves crumbled
1/4 cup tomato paste
2 cups halved grape tomatoes or 1 16-ounce can
 diced tomatoes, including juice
1 15-ounce can cannellini beans, rinsed and
 drained
2 quarts (8 cups) chicken or vegetable stock or
 broth
1 small zucchini, diced
1/4 pound green beans, cut in 1-inch lengths
1/2 cup uncooked quinoa, rinsed and drained
1/2 bunch kale, leaves removed and roughly
 chopped
1 tablespoon chopped parsley
salt and freshly ground black pepper to taste

Heat the olive oil in a heavy soup pot over medium-high heat, and sauté the onion for two minutes. Add the shallot, celery, garlic and bay leaf and cook until the celery is tender, about 5 minutes. Add the thyme, rosemary and tomato paste. Cook, stirring to blend, for two more minutes. Add the tomatoes, beans and stock, and bring the mixture to a boil.

Reduce heat to simmering. Add the zucchini, green beans and quinoa, and simmer until quinoa is tender, about 20 minutes. Add the kale and parsley, and cook until the kale is tender, about 5 minutes. Season with salt and pepper and serve. 10 servings.

Lentil Quinoa Soup

Based on a French recipe, this filling, flavorful soup combines lentils and quinoa for a richly satisfying meal.

4 cups chicken or vegetable stock or broth
4 cups water
1 pound dried lentils, washed and picked over
1 cup uncooked quinoa, rinsed and drained
2 medium turnips*, peeled and diced
2 medium onions, diced
2 large tomatoes, peeled, seeded and diced
2 large carrots, peeled and diced
1/4 cup olive oil
3 cloves garlic, peeled and minced
1 teaspoon dried oregano
salt and freshly ground pepper to taste

In a large soup pot, combine the broth and water to a boil over medium high heat. Add the other ingredients, bring the soup to a boil and reduce the heat to simmering. Cover and simmer over low heat for about an hour, or until lentils are tender. 10 to 12 servings.

Note about turnips: I know, I know; many of us fear cooked turnips. But the thing is, diced turnips in soups and stews are far superior to their spud counterparts. Everyone will think they *are*, in fact, potatoes. Turnips absorb some of the broth as they cook, but unlike potatoes they hold their shape and won't fall apart after a long simmer. Give turnips a try, and let me know what you think.

Quinoa Corn Chowder

I might as well tell you up front that this heavenly soup contains a cup of cream, shredded cheese and bacon. Thank goodness it also has a generous portion of healthy quinoa to offset the guilt.

2 tablespoons olive oil
1 large onion, chopped
4 cups fresh or frozen, thawed corn kernels
4 cups chicken or vegetable stock or broth
3/4 cup uncooked quinoa, rinsed and drained
1 teaspoon salt
1/4 teaspoon freshly ground black pepper
1 cup grated Muenster cheese
1 cup heavy cream
dash of hot pepper sauce
6 strips bacon, cooked and crumbled (optional)

In a large, heavy pot, heat the olive oil over medium heat. Add the onion and cook, stirring often, until translucent, about 4 minutes. Add the corn, stock, quinoa, salt and pepper and heat until almost boiling. Reduce heat to low and simmer for 20 minutes or until quinoa is tender.

Transfer half of the soup to a food processor or blender and puree. Return the blended mixture to the pot. Add the cheese, a little at a time, stirring and melting completely before adding more. Then add the cream very slowly, stirring constantly. Heat for a few more minutes, add the hot pepper sauce and check the seasonings. Ladle the soup into bowls and, if you like, sprinkle the crumbled bacon over each bowl. 6 to 8 servings.

Vegetable Quinoa Soup

This hearty recipe makes enough soup for a crowd, and its short cooking time keeps the vegetables bright and tender.

2 tablespoons olive oil
1 large onion, chopped
1 large shallot, chopped
1 clove garlic, peeled and minced
2 medium leeks, white and light green parts only, thinly sliced
1 1/2 cups uncooked quinoa, rinsed and drained
3 cups water
3 quarts vegetable or chicken stock or broth
2 large stalks celery, chopped
3 large carrots, scraped and sliced
2 medium turnips, peeled and chopped
1 medium sweet potato, peeled and chopped
1 tablespoon lemon juice
salt and freshly ground black pepper to taste
1/2 cup chopped flat-leaf parsley (optional)

In a large soup pot, heat the olive oil over medium heat. Add the onion, shallot, garlic, and leeks and sauté until tender. Add the quinoa and continue cooking, stirring occasionally, until the onion is lightly browned. Add the water and simmer for 10 minutes. Add the stock, celery, carrots, turnips, sweet potato and lemon juice and simmer 25-30 minutes, or until vegetables are tender. Add salt and pepper to taste. Garnish with chopped parsley before serving, if desired. 12 servings.

Creamy Mushroom Quinoa Soup

Quinoa, leeks, shallots and thyme enhance the fresh mushroom flavor of this simple, creamy soup.

3 thick slices bacon, diced
1 large leek, white and light green part only,
thinly sliced
1 large shallot, diced
2 cloves garlic, minced
1 large stalk celery, diced
1 pound button mushrooms, cleaned and sliced
1/4 cup Cognac
6 cups beef stock or broth
1 sprig fresh thyme or 1/4 teaspoon dried thyme
1/2 cup uncooked quinoa, rinsed and drained
1/2 cup half and half
salt and freshly ground black pepper to taste
1/4 cup chopped parsley
freshly grated Parmesan cheese for garnish

Cook the bacon in a large soup pot over medium heat until it starts to brown. Add the leek, shallot and garlic. Stir and continue cooking until the leek is tender. Add the celery, mushrooms, cognac, stock and thyme and bring soup to a boil. Add the quinoa and continue cooking for about 20 minutes, or until quinoa is tender. Add the half and half and cook until heated through; season to taste with salt and pepper. Serve garnished with parsley and Parmesan cheese. 6 servings.

Hearty Beef Quinoa Stew

Black quinoa thickens and flavors this old-fashioned, slow-cooked beef stew that's perfect for a chilly day.

2 tablespoons vegetable oil
1 1/2 pounds beef chuck, trimmed of visible fat and cut into 1-inch cubes
6 cups beef stock or broth, separated
1 16-ounce can Italian tomatoes, chopped
1/2 teaspoon dried thyme
2 bay leaves
freshly ground black pepper
3 thin carrots, peeled and sliced
3 stalks celery, sliced
1 medium onion, chopped
1 large turnip, peeled and diced
3/4 cup uncooked black quinoa, rinsed and drained
3/4 cup thawed frozen green peas
salt and freshly ground black pepper

Heat the oil in a large skillet over medium high heat until it shimmers. Brown the beef in batches, and transfer to a large, heavy soup pot. Add 2 cups of the beef stock, the tomatoes, thyme, bay leaves and pepper and cook over medium heat, covered, for one hour. Add the remaining beef stock, carrots, celery, onion, turnip and quinoa. Cook for 1 more hour. Add the peas and simmer just until they are heated through. Remove the bay leaves, season with salt and pepper, and serve immediately. 6 to 8 servings.

SALADS

Quinoa Salad with Orange, Avocado and Toasted Pistachios

This bright green and orange salad is as pretty as it is delicious, with tangy-sweet citrus flavors balanced by fluffy quinoa and creamy avocado.

1 head butter lettuce, washed, dried and torn in pieces
2 fresh navel oranges, peeled and sectioned
1 avocado, peeled and cut in 1/2-inch cubes
1 1/2 cups cooked quinoa
3 tablespoons orange juice
1 tablespoon fresh lemon juice
1 tablespoon honey
1 teaspoon grated lemon peel
3 tablespoons olive oil
salt and freshly ground black pepper to taste
1/2 cup toasted pistachios

In a salad bowl, combine the lettuce, oranges, avocado and quinoa and toss gently to combine. In a small bowl, whisk together the orange juice, lemon juice, honey, lemon peel and olive oil. Drizzle the dressing over the salad (you may not need it all) and season with salt and pepper. Top with toasted pistachios and serve. 4 servings.

Crunchy Thai Quinoa Salad with Peanut Ginger Dressing

Chow mein noodles, Napa cabbage, carrots and cashews add crunch to this Asian-style salad.

For the dressing:
1/4 cup creamy peanut butter
1 tablespoon honey
3 tablespoons tamari or soy sauce
2 teaspoons freshly grated ginger
1 tablespoon olive oil
1 tablespoon red wine vinegar
1 teaspoon sesame oil

For the salad:
2 cups cooked quinoa
2 cups shredded Napa cabbage
1 cup shelled, steamed edamame beans
1 cup crispy chow mein noodles
1 red bell pepper, seeded and thinly sliced
1/2 cup shredded carrots
1/2 cup chopped cilantro
2 green onions, thinly sliced
1/2 cup chopped honey-roasted cashews

Combine the peanut butter and honey in a small saucepan over medium heat and cook, stirring, until creamy. Stir in the tamari sauce, ginger, olive oil, vinegar and sesame oil, and reserve.

In a large bowl, combine the quinoa, cabbage, edamame, chow mein noodles, red bell pepper, carrots, cilantro and green onions. Drizzle with dressing and garnish with cashews. 6 servings.

Quinoa with Summer Tomatoes, Corn and Basil

Quinoa highlights the incomparable flavors of home-grown tomatoes and fresh sweet corn in this easy salad recipe, perfect for a summer picnic.

2 cups cooked quinoa
2 large ripe tomatoes, cut in small dice
kernels from 3 ears fresh, steamed sweet corn
6 ounces fresh mozzarella cheese, cut in small
  dice
16 fresh basil leaves, thinly sliced, divided
2 tablespoons olive oil
1 tablespoon Balsamic vinegar
salt and freshly ground black pepper to taste

In a large serving bowl, gently combine the quinoa, tomatoes, corn, mozzarella and half the basil. Whisk together the olive oil and Balsamic vinegar and drizzle over the salad. Season with salt and pepper to taste and stir gently. Top with the remaining basil. 4 servings.

Quinoa Spinach Salad with Orange Dressing

This updated take on the classic recipe combines warm quinoa, fresh spinach, crunchy bacon and a sweet-sour dressing.

For the dressing:
3 tablespoons olive oil
2 tablespoons orange juice
1 tablespoon red wine vinegar
1 tablespoon maple syrup
1 garlic clove, peeled and minced
1/2 teaspoon salt
1/8 teaspoon pepper
1 green onion, finely minced

For the salad:
2 cups water
1/2 teaspoon salt
1 cup uncooked quinoa, rinsed and drained
1/2 pound fresh baby spinach leaves
4 slices bacon, cooked, drained and crumbled

Whisk the dressing ingredients together in a small bowl and reserve.

In a medium saucepan, combine the water and salt and bring to a boil; add quinoa. Reduce heat; cover and simmer for 15 minutes or until quinoa is tender. Remove from heat and fluff with a fork.

In a large bowl, combine the warm quinoa and spinach. Drizzle the dressing over and toss to coat. Sprinkle with crumbled bacon. 6 servings.

Lemon Quinoa Salad with Crisp Vegetables

Crunchy vegetables pair with tender quinoa in this year-round salad topped with a lemony mustard dressing.

For the salad:
8 medium red radishes, thinly sliced
1 small jicama (about 12 ounces) peeled, quartered and cut in 1/4-inch slices
2 medium carrots, peeled and cut in 1/4-inch diagonal slices
2 stalks celery, strings removed and cut in 1/4-inch diagonal slices
1 medium fennel bulb, cored, halved and cut in 1/4-inch slices
1 yellow bell pepper, cored, seeded and thinly sliced
2 cups cooked quinoa
finely grated zest of 1 lemon

For the dressing:
2 tablespoons fresh lemon juice
1/3 cup olive oil
1 tablespoon sugar
1 garlic clove, peeled and minced
2 teaspoons Dijon mustard
salt and freshly ground black pepper to taste

Combine the sliced radishes, jicama, carrots, celery and fennel in a large bowl and cover with ice water. Refrigerate for about 1 hour, or until crisp.

Meanwhile, whisk together the lemon juice, olive oil, sugar, garlic, Dijon mustard, salt and pepper in a small bowl and reserve.

Drain and dry the vegetables, and combine them with the yellow bell pepper strips in a salad bowl. Fluff the quinoa with a fork and toss with the vegetables. Whisk the dressing and drizzle it over the salad. Season with salt and pepper. 4 servings.

Quinoa Green Bean Salad with Crispy Shallots

A marinated salad pairs quinoa with tender green beans and sautéed mushrooms, topped with golden brown fried shallots.

For the dressing:
2 tablespoons sherry vinegar
1 tablespoon Balsamic vinegar
1 medium shallot, peeled and minced
1 garlic clove, peeled and minced
1/2 teaspoon thyme leaves
1/4 cup olive oil

For the salad:
1/2 pound fresh green beans, ends trimmed
2 cups cooked quinoa
1 tablespoon butter
1/4 pound mushrooms of your choice, thinly
   sliced
3 large shallots
1 cup flour
1/4 teaspoon salt
1/4 teaspoon freshly ground black pepper
1/4 teaspoon paprika
1 cup vegetable oil
3 tablespoons salted toasted hazelnuts, coarsely
   chopped
salt and freshly ground black pepper to taste

To make the dressing, whisk the sherry and
Balsamic vinegar with the minced shallot, garlic
and thyme in a medium bowl. Whisk in the extra-
virgin olive oil; reserve.

In a large pot of boiling salted water, cook the green beans until crisp-tender, about 5 minutes; drain. Rinse the beans under cold water and pat dry. Toss the green beans and quinoa with the dressing and reserve.

In a medium skillet over medium high, heat the butter until it melts. Add the mushrooms and cook over high heat, stirring, until browned. Add to the green beans and stir gently to combine. (If you prefer a cold salad, cover and refrigerate the mixture for at least 2 hours or overnight before continuing.)

About 20 minutes before serving, peel the shallots and cut crosswise in thin, round slices. In a small bowl, combine the flour with the salt, pepper and paprika. Toss the sliced shallots with the flour mixture, separating them into rings. Transfer the shallots to a strainer and tap off the excess flour. Heat the oil in a medium saucepan. Add the shallots to the hot oil and fry over high heat, stirring, until golden, about 4 minutes. Using a slotted spoon, transfer the fried shallots to paper towels to drain thoroughly.

Season the green bean-quinoa mixture with salt and pepper to taste and divide evenly among six plates. Top with the fried shallots and toasted hazelnuts. 6 servings.

Black Bean, Corn, Quinoa and Avocado Salad

The flavors of the Southwest blend in this simple salad topped with a fresh lime-chipotle dressing.

For the dressing:
1/3 cup olive oil
1/4 cup fresh lime juice
1 tablespoon finely chopped green chiles
1/4 teaspoon salt
1/4 teaspoon freshly ground black pepper

For the salad:
1 cup fresh or frozen corn, cooked
1 cup cooked quinoa
1 15-ounce can black beans, rinsed and drained
1 cup diced tomatoes
1 tablespoon finely minced green onion
1 avocado, diced
1 small head butter lettuce, leaves separated
1/3 chopped fresh cilantro (or more or less to suit your taste)

To make the dressing, whisk together the olive oil, lime juice, chiles, salt and pepper in a small bowl.

Combine the corn, quinoa, beans, tomatoes, onion and avocados in a large bowl. Drizzle with the dressing and toss gently. Arrange lettuce leaves on four plates, divide the salad evenly among the plates and sprinkle with cilantro. 4 servings.

Greek Quinoa Salad

Quinoa pairs perfectly with the classic flavors of cucumbers, tomatoes and black olives, topped off with a zesty, lemon-oregano dressing.

For the dressing:
the juice of 1 lemon
2 tablespoons olive oil
1/4 teaspoon ground cumin
1/4 teaspoon dried oregano
1/2 teaspoon salt
1/4 teaspoon freshly ground black pepper

For the salad:
2 cups cooked quinoa, seasoned with salt and
   freshly ground black pepper
1/2 English cucumber, peeled, halved and sliced
1/2 cup cherry tomatoes, halved
1/2 red bell pepper, seeded and chopped
1/2 green bell pepper, seeded and chopped
1/4 cup sliced black olives
2 tablespoons chopped fresh parsley
1 tablespoon chopped fresh mint
4 ounces feta cheese, crumbled (optional)

In a small bowl, whisk together the dressing ingredients.

In a serving bowl, combine the quinoa, cucumber, tomatoes, peppers, olives, parsley and mint. Drizzle the dressing over the salad and stir gently to combine. Top with crumbled feta cheese, if desired. 6 servings.

Quinoa Autumn Salad with Apples, Red Pear, Dried Cherries and Toasted Pecans

When autumn apples are at their prime, this salad satisfies with a rich blend of quinoa and greens topped with a homemade vinaigrette.

For the dressing:
1/2 cup olive oil
2 tablespoons Balsamic vinegar
1 teaspoon Dijon mustard
1 teaspoon honey
1/2 teaspoon salt
1/4 teaspoon freshly ground black pepper

For the salad:
2 cups mixed greens
1 cup baby spinach
2 cups cooked quinoa
2 medium Granny Smith apples, cored, thinly
    sliced and roughly chopped
1 medium red pear, cored and sliced
1/3 cup dried cherries
1/4 cup chopped, toasted pecans

Combine the dressing ingredients in a small bowl and whisk until well blended; reserve.

Arrange the greens and spinach on six plates. Fluff the quinoa with a fork and divide it evenly among the plates. Divide the apples and pear slices evenly among plates and sprinkle dried cherries and chopped pecans. Drizzle each salad with the vinaigrette and serve. 6 servings.

Quinoa Salad with Edamame, Green Beans and Cherry Tomatoes

Bright and colorful, this salad is quick to prepare and makes an easy side dish or light lunch.

For the dressing:
1/3 cup olive oil
2 tablespoons Balsamic vinegar
1 teaspoon sugar
1/2 teaspoon Worcestershire sauce
1/2 teaspoon salt
1/4 teaspoon freshly ground black pepper
1 garlic clove, minced

1/2 pound green beans, cut in thirds
1 cup shelled edamame, cooked and cooled
1 cup cooked quinoa
1 pint cherry tomatoes, halved
1/4 cup torn fresh basil leaves
salt and freshly ground pepper to taste

Whisk together the dressing ingredients in a small bowl and reserve.

In a steamer basket over boiling water, cook the green beans until crisp-tender, about 5 minutes. Drain and cover with ice water for 5 minutes to cool; drain again. In a large serving dish, combine the green beans, edamame and cooked quinoa and drizzle with dressing to taste. Add the cherry tomatoes and basil leaves and stir gently. Taste and add more dressing, if needed. Sprinkle with salt and pepper and serve, or cover and refrigerate before serving. 6 servings.

Shrimp Quinoa Salad with Lemon Dressing

Perfect for an elegant lunch, this simple salad is served on lettuce leaves and topped with a homemade lemon-honey dressing.

For the dressing:
3 tablespoons fresh lemon juice
1 teaspoon honey
1/2 teaspoon dried oregano
1/2 teaspoon salt
1/4 teaspoon freshly ground black pepper
1/4 cup olive oil

For the salad:
3/4 pound large raw shrimp, peeled
1 1/2 cups cooked quinoa
1 medium tomato, cut in 1/2-inch pieces
1 small avocado, cut in 1/2-inch pieces
1 ounce mild chevre cheese, gently crumbled
4 large Boston lettuce leaves

To make the dressing, whisk together lemon juice, honey, oregano, salt and pepper in a medium bowl. Slowly whisk in the olive oil and reserve.

Fill a large pan or bowl with water and ice and reserve. Set a large saucepan of lightly salted water over medium-high heat. Bring to a boil. Add shrimp and cook until shrimp turn pink, about 1 minute. Drain and add the shrimp to the ice water. After 5 minutes, drain the shrimp.

In a medium bowl, mix together quinoa, shrimp, tomatoes and avocado. Drizzle with the dressing and toss gently. Add the crumbled chevre and stir gently.

To serve, arrange a lettuce leaf on each of four plates and divide the salad evenly among the plates. 4 servings.

Best Quinoa Cole Slaw

Quinoa's tender texture is a welcome addition to this crunchy, old-fashioned cole slaw recipe, which gets its sweet-tangy flavor from a dash of pickle juice.

For the dressing:
2/3 cup mayonnaise
1 tablespoon Balsamic vinegar
2 teaspoons sugar
1/4 teaspoon salt
1/4 cup sweet pickle juice from the pickle jar
1/2 teaspoon ground pepper
1/2 teaspoon dry mustard

For the salad:
3 cups shredded green cabbage
1 cup cooked quinoa
1 cup shredded red cabbage
3 medium carrots, peeled and shredded

Whisk together the dressing ingredients in a large bowl. Add the salad ingredients and toss gently. Serve at once or cover and refrigerate. 8 servings.

Crunchy Quinoa Veggie Salad with Minted Pesto

Perfect on a summer day, quinoa blends with snow peas, cucumbers, celery and red bell peppers tossed with a light, minted pesto dressing.

For the pesto:
3/4 cup loosely packed fresh basil leaves
3 tablespoons chopped fresh mint leaves
2 tablespoons chopped fresh parsley
1 garlic clove, peeled and crushed
3 tablespoons blanched almonds
2 tablespoons grated Parmesan cheese
2 to 3 tablespoons olive oil
salt and freshly ground black pepper to taste

For the salad:
1 cup cooked, cooled quinoa
1/4 pound snow peas, cut in 1/2 inch diagonal
   pieces and lightly steamed
1 English cucumber, peeled, halved, and sliced
1 red bell pepper, roasted, peeled and diced
1 avocado, peeled and cut in 1/2-inch cubes
1/3 cup finely diced celery

Put the basil, mint, parsley, garlic and almonds in a food processor. Blend at low speed until the ingredients are coarsely chopped. Add the cheese and half of the olive oil and blend again. Trickle in the remaining olive oil while blending on low speed. Stir in salt and pepper to taste. In a large bowl, toss together the quinoa, snow peas, cucumber, red pepper, avocado and celery. Add the pesto and stir until combined. 4 to 6 servings.

Quinoa Chopped Salad

This recipe is based on a salad I once enjoyed at an Atlanta restaurant. I liked the combination of flavors so much, I wrote down the ingredients as I ate...and ate...and ate. Crunchy lettuces, quinoa and fresh veggies are tossed with creamy Italian dressing and Gorgonzola cheese.

For the dressing:
1/2 cup best-quality mayonnaise
1/4 cup white vinegar
2 tablespoons honey
2 tablespoons grated Parmesan cheese
2 tablespoons grated Romano cheese
2 teaspoons lemon juice
1 teaspoon olive oil
1 garlic clove, minced
1/2 teaspoon dried Italian seasoning
1 teaspoon finely chopped parsley
salt and freshly ground black pepper to taste

For the salad:
1 medium head romaine lettuce, chopped
1 small head iceberg lettuce, chopped
1 15-ounce can garbanzo beans, drained and
  rinsed
1 cup cooked quinoa, room temperature
2 large tomatoes, chopped
1 avocado, peeled and cubed
1/2 cup torn basil leaves
1/4 cup pitted, sliced black olives
4 ounces Gorgonzola cheese, crumbled

To make the dressing, whisk together the ingredients in a small bowl until completely blended and reserve.

To make the salad, combine the lettuces, garbanzo beans, quinoa, tomatoes, avocado and basil leaves in a large bowl and toss gently. Add the black olives and Gorgonzola cheese and drizzle with the dressing (you may have extra). Toss gently to combine. 6 servings.

Creamy Red Potato and Quinoa Salad

This delicious variation on traditional potato salad pairs nutty quinoa with oven-roasted potatoes and crunchy bacon.

3 pounds small red new potatoes, scrubbed and quartered
2 tablespoons extra virgin olive oil
2 shallots, peeled and chopped
1/2 teaspoon salt
1/4 teaspoon freshly ground black pepper
1 cup sour cream
2/3 cup mayonnaise
1 cup cooked quinoa
6 slices bacon, cooked and crumbled

Preheat the oven to 350 degrees F. Toss the potatoes in the olive oil and spread on a baking sheet. Bake for 15 minutes, remove from the oven and sprinkle the shallots on top. Return to the oven and continue baking for 10 to 15 minutes, or until potatoes are tender and shallots are lightly browned. Sprinkle with salt and pepper and cool.

In a large serving bowl, combine the sour cream, mayonnaise, quinoa and bacon. Add the potato-shallot mixture and stir gently to combine. Check seasonings and cool salad to room temperature, stirring occasionally. Serve or cover and chill in the refrigerator. 8 servings.

Tuna Salad with Quinoa, Tomatoes, Avocado and Basil

Rich and flavorful, this recipe updates traditional mayo-based tuna salad with cool tomatoes, diced avocado and the incomparable flavor of quinoa.

2 cups cooked quinoa
8 ounces canned albacore tuna, drained
1 cup cooked or drained, canned garbanzo beans
1 cup grape or small cherry tomatoes, halved
1 avocado, peeled and cubed
1/4 cup creamy Italian dressing (or more or less
   to suit your taste)
salt and freshly ground black pepper to taste
1/2 cup fresh, chopped basil leaves

In a large bowl, combine the quinoa, tuna, beans, tomatoes and avocado. Stir gently. Drizzle with the dressing and stir gently. Sprinkle with the salt and pepper and add the fresh basil. Stir gently to combine and serve immediately. 6 servings.

Quinoa Taco Salad with Lime-Cilantro Dressing

Crispy, oven-baked tortilla strips add crunch to this hearty salad, topped with a fresh-made cilantro dressing.

For the tortilla strips:
4 corn tortillas, cut in 1/4-inch strips
2 tablespoons olive oil

For the dressing:
1/4 cup lime juice
1 clove garlic, minced
1/2 cup fresh cilantro, chopped
1/3 cup olive oil
1 teaspoon honey
1 teaspoon ground cumin
1 teaspoon salt

For the salad:
1 1/2 cups cooked quinoa
1 15-ounce can black beans, drained and rinsed
1 cup fresh or frozen corn, cooked
1 tomato, seeded and diced
1/2 red onion, diced
1 Anaheim chile, seeded and diced
1 jalapeño, seeded and diced (optional)
1 avocado, diced

Preheat oven to 450 degrees F. On a rimmed baking sheet, toss tortilla strips with olive oil; season with salt. Bake for 5 minutes or until lightly browned and crispy. Remove from oven and drain on paper towels.

To make the dressing, combine the lime juice, garlic, cilantro, olive oil, honey, cumin and salt in a food processor or blender and process until the mixture is smooth.

In a large bowl, combine the cooked quinoa, black beans, corn, tomato, red onion, chiles, jalapeño and avocado .

Drizzle the dressing over the salad and toss gently to combine. To serve, divide the salad among four plates and top with tortilla strips. 4 servings.

Four Bean Quinoa Salad

Colorful red or black quinoa pairs beautifully with a quartet of beans in this popular picnic salad.

1 14.5-ounce can kidney beans, rinsed and drained
1 14.5-ounce can garbanzo beans, rinsed and drained
1 14.5-ounce can black beans, rinsed and drained
2 cups lightly steamed green beans, cut in 2-inch pieces
1 cup cooked red or black quinoa (or 1/2 cup of each)
2 celery stalks, diced
juice and zest of one lemon
4 teaspoons olive oil
salt and freshly ground black pepper to taste
1/4 cup chopped parsley

Combine kidney beans, garbanzo beans, black beans, green beans, quinoa and celery in a medium bowl. In a small bowl, whisk together the lemon juice and olive oil. Drizzle the dressing over the bean mixture and season with salt and pepper. Just before serving, sprinkle with chopped parsley. 8 servings.

DINNERS

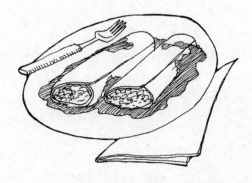

Hearty Quinoa Meatballs in Marinara Sauce

Forget heavy meatballs. Cooked quinoa replaces the usual bread crumbs, and the result is a meatball with a light, tender bite. This recipe calls for red quinoa, which blends nicely with the meat mixture.

3 tablespoons olive oil
1 small onion, minced
2 cloves garlic, minced
3/4 cups mushrooms, finely chopped
2 tablespoons Balsamic vinegar
1 cup cooked red quinoa
1/2 cup fresh basil, finely sliced
1 pound ground chuck
1/2 pound ground pork
1/3 cup tomato paste
2 eggs
1 tablespoon Worcestershire sauce
1/2 cup shredded mozzarella cheese
1 1/2 teaspoons finely crumbled dried oregano
1/2 teaspoon salt
1/4 teaspoon freshly ground black pepper
4 cups marinara sauce
1 pound linguine
grated Parmesan cheese

Preheat the oven to 400 degrees F and lightly grease a baking sheet.

Heat the olive oil in a medium skillet over medium heat. Sauté the onion until lightly browned, about five minutes. Add the garlic and continue cooking for two minutes, until fragrant. Add the mushrooms and continue to cook, stirring occasionally, for five minutes. Add the Balsamic vinegar and increase heat to high. Cook, stirring constantly, until most of the liquid cooks away. Remove from the heat and let the mixture cool in the pan for five minutes.

In a large bowl, combine the cooled mushroom mixture with the quinoa, basil, ground chuck, ground pork, tomato paste, eggs, Worcestershire sauce, cheese, oregano, salt and pepper. Mix gently with your hands until well combined. Gently form the mixture into 1 1/2-inch meatballs, and arrange on the prepared baking sheet. Bake for 20 to 25 minutes, or until no longer pink in the center.

While the meatballs are baking, boil a pot of water for the linguine. In a separate large pot, heat the marinara sauce to simmering over medium heat. When the meatballs are done cooking, cool for 5 minutes and drop them into the pot of marinara sauce. Cook the linguine in the boiling water until it is tender, and drain. Serve the pasta in warmed bowls and ladle some of the sauce and meatballs over it. Sprinkle with grated Parmesan cheese. 6 servings.

Quinoa Ranch Casserole

Kid-friendly ranch dressing enlivens this blend of mild summer squash, chicken and quinoa, and adults will love it, too.

1 tablespoon butter
1 large or 2 small summer squash, cut in 1/4-inch slices
1 cup sliced mushrooms
3 cups cooked quinoa
salt and freshly ground black pepper to taste
3 cups cooked, chopped chicken
1/3 cup ranch dressing
1/2 cup shredded Cheddar cheese

Preheat oven to 375 degrees F and lightly grease a 2 quart casserole dish. Melt the butter in a nonstick skillet over medium-high heat. Add the squash and cook, stirring occasionally, for five minutes. Add the mushrooms and continue cooking until squash is tender; reserve.

Season the cooked quinoa with salt and pepper, and spread it evenly in the casserole dish. Add the chicken next in an even layer and drizzle with the ranch dressing. Top with the sautéed squash and mushroom mixture and sprinkle the Cheddar cheese evenly over the top. Cover and cook for 25 minutes, or until hot and bubbly. Remove lid or foil and cook for an additional 5 minutes. 6 servings.

Quinoa, Black Bean and Green Chile Enchiladas

Corn, quinoa and black beans make a satisfying filling for these easy baked enchiladas.

2 cups cooked quinoa
1 15.5-ounce can black beans, rinsed and
  drained
2 cups cooked fresh or frozen corn
2 15.5-ounce cans green chile enchilada sauce
2 cups shredded cheese, divided
12 small flour tortillas
shredded lettuce
chopped tomato
sour cream

Preheat the oven to 350 degrees F and grease a 9-by 13-inch baking dish.

In a large skillet over medium heat, combine the quinoa, black beans, corn and one can of the enchilada sauce. Heat for five minutes, stir in one cup shredded cheese and stir just until cheese melts. Remove from heat and cool for five minutes. Spoon a generous portion of filling into each of the tortillas, rolling to close. Place in a baking dish/pan, seam side down. Drizzle with remaining enchilada sauce and 1 cup shredded cheese. Bake for 20 minutes, or until cheese is melted and sauce is bubbling. Serve topped with lettuce, tomato and sour cream. 12 enchiladas.

Quinoa Bacon Broccoli Bake

This quick and easy casserole can be assembled in minutes. Just add a green salad and dinner is done.

1 cup uncooked quinoa, rinsed and drained
2 cups chicken or vegetable stock
2 tablespoons butter
2 tablespoons flour
1/2 cup half and half
1/2 cup milk
2 cups shredded Cheddar cheese, divided
1/4 teaspoon salt
1/4 teaspoon black pepper
1 cup steamed broccoli florets
3 slices bacon, cooked and crumbled

Preheat the oven to 350 degrees F and grease a 1 1/2 quart casserole dish.

Heat the quinoa and stock in a large saucepan over medium high heat. Bring to a boil, then cover, reduce heat, and simmer for about 15 minutes, or until quinoa is tender and all of the liquid has been absorbed.

While the quinoa is cooking, melt the butter in a large nonstick skillet over medium heat. Whisk in the flour and cook for two minutes. Slowly pour in the half and half and milk, and whisk vigorously. Reduce heat to low and gradually add 1 1/2 cups of the cheese, stirring with each addition. Season with the salt and pepper and add the cooked quinoa, stirring to combine.

Pour half of the quinoa mixture in the casserole dish and top with the steamed broccoli and bacon. Top with the remaining quinoa mixture and sprinkle with the remaining 1/2 cup of cheese.

Bake for 15 to 20 minutes, or until the mixture is hot and bubbling and the cheese is melted. 4 to 6 servings.

Quinoa con Pollo (Quinoa and Chicken)

The meat in chicken thighs is especially flavorful, and it pairs well with quinoa and peas in this simmered one-skillet dinner.

2 cups uncooked quinoa, rinsed and drained
6 skinless, boneless chicken thighs
2 teaspoons salt, divided
3 tablespoons olive oil
1 medium onion, chopped
3 cloves garlic, minced
2 tablespoons tomato paste
2 teaspoons paprika
1/2 teaspoon freshly ground black pepper
1/4 teaspoon cayenne pepper
1/2 red bell pepper, cut in 1-inch pieces
3 1/2 cups chicken stock
1 cup frozen green peas

Put the quinoa in a saucepan and cover with water and bring to a boil over medium-high heat. Simmer for five minutes and strain.

Sprinkle the chicken thighs with 1 teaspoon of the salt. Heat 2 tablespoons olive oil in a large skillet over medium high heat and fry the chicken, pressing down with a spatula, for about 3 minutes on each side until well browned but still moist inside. Remove the chicken, cut in 1-inch pieces and reserve.

Add the remaining olive oil to the pan, heat over medium heat and sauté onions for two minutes.

Add the garlic and continue cooking until the onions are translucent. Add the drained quinoa and cook for five minutes. (The mixture will be dry.) Add the chicken pieces, tomato paste, paprika, black pepper, cayenne, red bell pepper and chicken stock. Bring to a boil, reduce the heat to medium-low, cover and simmer until the quinoa is tender.

Remove the lid, add the green peas and cook until liquid is absorbed and peas are tender. Adjust the seasonings, if necessary, and fluff with a fork before serving. 4 to 6 servings.

Quinoa Pork "Fried Rice"

This updated take on traditional fried rice is my family's #1 favorite way to enjoy quinoa. Serve it hot from the skillet and see if you agree.

4 strips bacon, diced
1/2 pound lean pork, cut in 1/2-inch cubes
2 stalks celery, cut in 1/2-inch diagonal slices
1/2 cup chopped onion
1/4 pound snow peas, trimmed and cut in 1-inch
    diagonal slices
3 cups cooked quinoa
1 tablespoon tamari or low-sodium soy sauce
2 eggs, lightly beaten

In a skillet over medium heat, cook the bacon for five minutes until it just begins to brown. Add the pork, celery and onion and continue cooking until the bacon is browned and the vegetables are tender. Add the snow peas and cook for 1 minute. Add the quinoa and soy sauce and cook for 3 minutes, stirring constantly.

Pour the eggs over the mixture in a stream, stirring constantly, and cook just until eggs are cooked. Remove from heat and serve at once. 6 servings.

BBQ Chicken Quinoa and Corn

Another family-pleasing favorite, this recipe combines roasted chicken with quinoa, corn and a creamy barbeque sauce.

1 cup uncooked quinoa, rinsed and drained
2 cups chicken broth
salt and freshly ground black pepper to taste
1 small rotisserie chicken, boned and chopped
1/2 cup barbeque sauce, divided
1/4 cup sour cream
1 cup fresh or frozen cooked corn kernels
1/2 cup black beans, drained and rinsed
1/2 cup shredded sharp Cheddar cheese
1/4 cup chopped fresh cilantro

Combine the quinoa with the chicken broth in a saucepan and bring to a boil over medium-high heat. Lower the heat to medium-low, cover and cook until quinoa is tender, about 20 minutes. Season to taste with salt and pepper.

In a medium bowl, toss the chopped chicken with 1/4 cup of the barbeque sauce until pieces are coated. In a small bowl, whisk together the remaining barbeque sauce and sour cream; reserve. Heat the corn and black beans and keep warm.

To serve, divide the warm quinoa among four plates. Top with the shredded chicken, corn, black beans and shredded cheese. Drizzle with the sour cream/barbeque sauce mixture and garnish with chopped cilantro. 4 servings.

Quinoa Burrito Bowls

Highlighting all of the flavors we love without any fuss, burrito bowls are great because everyone can add the ingredients they especially like.

1 tablespoon olive oil
1/4 cup minced onion
1 clove garlic, peeled and minced
2 15 ounce cans pinto beans, rinsed and drained
1/2 cup water
4 tablespoons chopped fresh cilantro, divided
1/4 teaspoon chili powder
pinch of cayenne pepper
2 limes
salt and freshly ground black pepper to taste
3 cups cooked red quinoa
1 cup shredded lettuce

Topping suggestions:
grated Colby or Monterey Jack cheese
sour cream
Pico de Gallo or salsa
chopped fresh tomatoes
guacamole
steamed corn
hot sauce
diced avocado
corn chips

Heat the olive oil in a large pot over medium heat. Sauté the onions until they are lightly browned, about five minutes. Add the garlic and continue cooking for two minutes, until fragrant. Add the beans, water, 2 tablespoons of the chopped cilantro, chili powder and cayenne pepper. Bring the beans to a boil and reduce heat to medium low. Let the beans simmer for 15 minutes till the liquid is mostly evaporated. Stir in the juice of one lime and season to taste with salt and pepper.

Fluff the quinoa with a fork and add the remaining 2 tablespoons chopped cilantro and the juice from the remaining lime. Season with salt to taste.

To serve, divide the quinoa mixture between four bowls. Top with shredded lettuce followed by a generous spoonful of the bean mixture. Garnish with additional toppings. 4 servings.

Crispy Quinoa Chicken Tacos with Avocado

These crunchy tacos feature a chicken-quinoa-pinto bean filling enlivened with a squeeze of fresh lime.

2 cups chopped cooked chicken
1 cup cooked quinoa
1 15.5-ounce can pinto beans, drained
1 lime, cut in half
1/4 teaspoon salt
1/4 teaspoon freshly ground black pepper
1 ripe avocado, peeled and diced
1 medium tomato, diced
1 tablespoon fresh cilantro, chopped
12 crispy taco shells, warmed in the oven
shredded lettuce
shredded cheese
fresh pico de gallo or prepared salsa

In a large bowl, combine the chicken, quinoa and pinto beans. Squeeze the lime over the mixture and sprinkle with salt and pepper; stir to combine. Add avocado, tomato and cilantro and stir gently. Fill taco shells with mixture and top with shredded lettuce, shredded cheese and pico de gallo or salsa. 12 tacos.

Asian Ginger Quinoa with Snow Peas

Fresh ginger pairs with quinoa and crispy vegetables for a quick-simmered dinner. Accompany with dumplings or spring rolls, and don't forget the chopsticks.

1 1/2 cups chicken or vegetable broth
3/4 cup uncooked quinoa, rinsed and drained
2 tablespoons rice vinegar
2 tablespoons plum sauce
2 garlic cloves, minced
1 teaspoon minced fresh gingerroot
1 teaspoon sesame oil
1/4 teaspoon salt
1 cup fresh snow peas, trimmed and halved
1/2 medium sweet red pepper, cut in 1- by 1/4-inch strips
1/2 cup sliced water chestnuts, chopped

In a large skillet over medium-high heat, combine the broth, quinoa, rice vinegar, plum sauce, garlic, ginger, sesame oil and salt; bring to a boil. Reduce heat; cover and simmer for about 15 minutes, or until quinoa is cooked and most of the water is absorbed. Stir in the snow peas, red bell pepper and water chestnuts. Cover and cook for 3-4 minutes, or until snow peas are tender. Fluff with a fork and serve. 4 servings.

Wild Salmon with Quinoa and Green Beans

An orange-Balsamic glaze flavors tender wild salmon filets, which are paired with ginger quinoa and crisp-tender green beans.

2 tablespoon Balsamic vinegar, divided
2 tablespoon orange juice
1 1/2 tablespoon tamari or low sodium soy sauce
2 teaspoons teaspoon honey
4 wild salmon filets (about 1 pound)
3/4 pound fresh green beans, ends trimmed
2 teaspoons olive oil
1/2 teaspoon fresh grated ginger
1 cup cooked quinoa
1 teaspoon sesame oil

Preheat a grill or oven broiler.

In a small bowl, whisk together the Balsamic vinegar, orange juice, tamari or soy sauce and honey. Brush half of the mixture over the salmon filets, turning to coat, and reserve the rest.

Heat a pot of boiling water and cook the beans just until crisp-tender, about five minutes; drain.

In a large skillet, heat the olive oil over medium high heat until it begins to shimmer. Add the green beans and ginger and cook, stirring constantly, for two minutes. Add the quinoa and remaining Balsamic vinegar mixture and continue cooking until heated through. Drizzle the sesame oil over the mixture and stir until combined. Remove from heat and keep warm.

Broil or grill the salmon filets until they flake easily and are opaque. Remove the skin from the filets. To serve, divide the green bean mixture among four heated plates and top each with a salmon filet. 4 servings.

Coconut Quinoa with Shrimp and Ginger

The nutty flavors of toasted coconut and quinoa are a match made in heaven, topped with zesty, quick-fried shrimp.

1 1/2 cups uncooked quinoa, rinsed and drained
3 cups chicken stock or broth
1/3 cup unsweetened coconut flakes
1 tablespoon olive oil
2/3 cup grated carrots
1/3 cup diced onion
1 teaspoon grated fresh ginger
1 clove garlic, peeled and minced
12 large shrimp, peeled and deveined
salt and freshly ground black pepper to taste
1 lime
1/4 cup fresh chopped cilantro

Heat the quinoa and stock in a large saucepan over medium high heat. Bring to a boil, then cover, reduce heat, and simmer for about 15 minutes, or until quinoa is tender and all of the liquid has been absorbed.

While the quinoa is cooking, heat a large nonstick skillet over medium heat and cook the coconut, stirring frequently, until the flakes turn light brown. Transfer the coconut to a small bowl and return the skillet to the stove. Heat the olive oil and cook the carrots and onions, stirring occasionally, until onion is opaque and carrots are tender. Add the ginger and garlic and cook for one to two minutes, or until garlic is fragrant. Transfer mixture to a small bowl and return skillet to stove. Add the shrimp and cook them, turning several times, until they are bright pink and opaque.

Fluff the cooked quinoa with a fork and toss it with the toasted coconut, carrot mixture and ginger mixture. Season to taste with salt and pepper.

To serve, divide the quinoa mixture among four warmed plates. Top with the shrimp, squeeze with the fresh line and garnish with chopped cilantro. 4 servings.

Jerk Chicken with Caribbean Quinoa

This recipe might sound like it's named for a bad boyfriend, but it gets its title from a spicy "jerk" seasoning blend. If you've ever eaten jerk pork, you'll love the sweet heat of this Jamaican-inspired chicken quinoa dish.

For the vinaigrette:
1 8-ounce can crushed pineapple in natural juice
3 tablespoons olive oil
2 tablespoons fresh lime juice

For the chicken:
1 cup uncooked quinoa, rinsed and drained
1 1/4 cups chicken stock or broth
2 1/2 tablespoons jerk seasoning blend
2 tablespoons olive oil
1 1/2 pounds boneless, skinless chicken cut in 1-inch wide strips
1 green onion, finely minced
2 tablespoons chopped cilantro
salt and freshly ground black pepper to taste

Drain 3 tablespoons of pineapple juice from the canned pineapple and pour it in a small bowl. Add the olive oil and lime juice and whisk to combine; reserve.

Heat the quinoa and stock in a large saucepan over medium high heat. Bring to a boil, then cover, reduce heat, and simmer for about 15 minutes, or until quinoa is tender and all of the liquid has been absorbed. Keep warm.

Combine the olive oil mixture and jerk seasoning blend in a large bowl. Pat the chicken pieces dry and add to the bowl, stirring to coat each piece evenly. Heat a large nonstick skillet over medium-high heat and cook the chicken for 3 to 4 minutes on each side, or until lightly browned and thoroughly cooked through.

Toss the quinoa with a fork and add 1/3 cup of the drained pineapple (reserve the rest for another use). Sprinkle with the green onion and cilantro, and stir until combined. Season with salt and pepper. Divide the quinoa mixture among 6 warmed plates and top with the cooked chicken. 6 servings.

Quinoa Crab Cakes

Would it be too bold to suggest that quinoa is the secret ingredient that's been missing in traditional crab cakes for all these years? Quinoa binds beautifully with the crabmeat for a cake that's crispy on the outside, and light and tender on the inside.

1/2 cup mayonnaise
1 egg, lightly beaten
2 teaspoons Dijon mustard
1 teaspoon seafood seasoning mix such as Old Bay ®
1 pound jumbo lump crabmeat, picked over
1/2 cup cooked quinoa
3 tablespoons canola oil
1 lemon, cut in wedges

Line a large baking sheet with parchment paper. Combine the mayonnaise, egg, mustard and seasoning mix in a large bowl and whisk until combined. Add the crabmeat and quinoa and toss gently with a fork just until mixed. Gently form the mixture in 8 patties, about 1 inch thick, and arrange on the baking sheet. Refrigerate for one hour.

In a large skillet, heat the oil over medium high until it shimmers. Add the crab cakes and cook until deeply golden and heated through, about 3 minutes per side. Serve with lemon wedges. 8 crab cakes, about 4 servings.

Asparagus with Quinoa, Pancetta and Leeks

With tender asparagus and crispy pancetta, this quick skillet meal is rich and flavorful.

1/4 pound pancetta (or substitute bacon) cut in
    1/4-inch dice
1 pound asparagus, trimmed and sliced in 2-inch
    pieces on the bias
1 large leek, white and pale green parts only,
    thoroughly washed and thinly sliced crosswise
2 cloves garlic, minced
zest of one lemon
1 cup cooked quinoa
1 tablespoon chopped Italian parsley
salt and freshly ground pepper to taste

In a large skillet over medium heat, sauté the pancetta or bacon, stirring frequently, until almost crisp. Add the asparagus and leek and sauté until the asparagus is just tender, about 3 to 4 minutes.

Add the garlic and lemon zest, and sauté for about 1 minute, until fragrant. Add the quinoa and parsley, and cook for one more minute. Season to taste with salt and pepper, and serve immediately. 4 servings.

Toasted Quinoa Pilaf with Scallops and Sugar Snap Peas

Browning the quinoa before cooking brings out its nutty flavor, which pairs beautifully with the creamy scallops and crunchy peas.

1 pound sea scallops
4 teaspoons tamari or low-sodium soy sauce, divided
1 1/2 cups uncooked quinoa, rinsed and drained
3 cups vegetable stock or broth
1 teaspoon salt
1 1/2 cups sugar snap peas, trimmed
1 tablespoon olive oil
1/4 cup rice vinegar
1 teaspoon sesame oil
1 teaspoon grated fresh ginger
2 green onions, thinly sliced
2 teaspoons canola oil
1/4 cup chopped fresh Italian parsley

Combine the scallops and 2 teaspoons of the tamari sauce in a medium bowl, and stir to coat. Reserve.

Heat a large nonstick skillet over medium-high heat. Add the quinoa and cook, stirring constantly for 4-5 minutes, until quinoa begins to darken. Remove from heat and add the stock or broth and salt. Stir to combine, cover and cook over medium heat for 15 minutes, or until all water is absorbed. Remove from heat and let stand covered for 5 minutes. Stir in sugar snap peas, re-cover and let stand 5 more minutes.

In a large bowl, whisk together the olive oil, the remaining 2 teaspoons tamari sauce, vinegar, sesame oil, and ginger. Add the quinoa-snap pea mixture and green onions, and fluff with a fork to combine.

In a large skillet, heat the canola oil over medium high heat until shimmering. Remove the scallops from the marinade and sauté until lightly browned and opaque, about 2 minutes per side. To serve, divide the quinoa mixture among four heated shallow bowls and top with the seared scallops. Garnish with chopped parsley. 4 servings.

Creamy Quinoa Polenta with Marinara Sauce

The ultimate comfort food, quinoa adds rich flavor and texture to warm polenta topped with a quick, homemade marinara sauce.

For the polenta:
4 cups chicken stock or broth, divided
1/2 cup uncooked quinoa, rinsed and drained
1/2 cup cornmeal
3 tablespoons unsalted butter
1 teaspoon salt
1/4 teaspoon freshly ground black pepper
1/4 cup grated Parmesan cheese

For the marinara sauce:
2 tablespoons olive oil
1 large onion, finely chopped
1 large portobello mushroom, chopped
3 cloves garlic, peeled and minced
2 14.5 ounce cans stewed tomatoes
1/2 teaspoon crushed red pepper flakes
1 teaspoon crushed dried oregano
salt and freshly ground black pepper to taste
1/4 cup shaved Parmesan cheese

In a small bowl whisk together 2 cups of the chicken stock with the quinoa, cornmeal and salt. Bring the remaining 2 cups water to a boil in a heavy saucepan. Stir the quinoa mixture into the boiling water, and continue stirring. Turn the heat to very low and cook the polenta for 40 minutes, stirring every 10 minutes to keep mixture smooth.

When the mixture is creamy, remove from the heat and add the butter, salt, and pepper. Gradually add the Parmesan cheese, stirring to combine thoroughly.

While the polenta is cooking, heat the olive oil in a large saucepan over medium heat and add the onions. Cook for about 5 minutes, stirring often, until softened. Stir in the chopped mushrooms and garlic and sauté for 5 minutes. Add the tomatoes, red pepper flakes and oregano. When the sauce comes to a boil turn the heat to low. Simmer the sauce for 30 minutes; season with salt and pepper to taste.

To serve, divide the polenta among 4 heated shallow bowls. Make a well in the center and ladle some of the marinara sauce over. Garnish with shaved Parmesan cheese. 4 servings.

Layered Quinoa Cheese Enchilada Bake

Easy to assemble and so delicious, you'll love the Mexican flavors in this simple casserole.

For the red enchilada sauce:
1 tablespoon olive oil
1 small onion, finely minced
2 cloves garlic, peeled and minced
3 tablespoons chili powder
1 tablespoon ground cumin
1 15-ounce can tomato sauce
1 cup chicken stock or broth
salt and freshly ground black pepper to taste

For the casserole:
1 cup uncooked quinoa, rinsed and drained
2 cups chicken broth
1/2 teaspoon salt
12 white corn tortillas
2 cups cheese

For the toppings:
diced fresh tomatoes
chopped avocados
sour cream
chopped cilantro

To make the sauce, heat the olive oil in a medium saucepan over medium-high heat. Add the onions and sauté for about 5 minutes, stirring often, until they have softened. Add the garlic, chili powder, and cumin and cook for one minute. Add the tomato sauce and chicken broth, stirring to combine, and bring the mixture to a boil. Reduce heat to low and simmer for 10 minutes. Season to taste with salt and pepper and reserve.

Heat the quinoa, broth and salt in a large saucepan over medium high heat. Bring to a boil, then cover, reduce heat, and simmer for about 15 minutes, or until quinoa is tender and all of the liquid has been absorbed.

Preheat the oven to 350 degrees F and grease a 3 quart casserole dish. Spread a layer of sauce on the bottom of the dish. Arrange 4 of the tortillas in a layer on top, followed by a layer of sauce, 1/3 of the quinoa and a layer of cheese. Repeat two times. Cook for 20 to 30 minutes, or until the cheese is hot and bubbly. Serve accompanied with chopped tomatoes, avocados, sour cream and cilantro. 6 servings.

Bacon Quinoa

This simple, delicious dish features two of my very favorite foods.

2 thick slices bacon, cut in 1/4-inch dice
1 small shallot, minced
1 cup uncooked quinoa, rinsed and drained
2 cups chicken stock or broth
1 tablespoon minced chives
1 tablespoon chopped parsley
salt and freshly ground black pepper to taste

Preheat the oven to 350 degrees F. In a medium saucepan, cook the bacon over moderately high heat until the fat has rendered, about 2 minutes. Add the shallot and cook, stirring a few times, until softened but not browned, about 1 minute. Add the quinoa and chicken stock and bring to a boil.

Cover and cook over low heat until the stock has been absorbed, about 20 minutes. Remove the quinoa from the heat and let stand, covered, for 5 minutes. Fluff with a fork and stir in the chives and parsley. Season with salt and pepper and serve. 4 servings.

SIDE DISHES

Baked French Onion Quinoa and Cauliflower

If you're a fan of golden, cheese-topped French Onion Soup, you'll love this flavorful baked quinoa gratin.

1 tablespoon butter
1 small onion, thinly sliced
3 cups cooked quinoa
1/2 large head cauliflower, chopped
2 cups beef stock or broth
1 clove garlic, minced
1/2 teaspoon salt
1/4 teaspoon freshly ground black pepper
1/3 cup minced fresh parsley
1 cup seasoned bread crumbs
1 1/2 cups shredded Gruyère cheese

Preheat oven to 350 degrees F and grease six 10-ounce ovenproof ramekin dishes. In a small skillet over medium heat, melt the butter and sauté the onion until tender and lightly browned. Remove from heat.

In a medium bowl, combine the quinoa, cauliflower, beef stock, garlic, sautéed onions, salt and pepper. Spoon mixture into ramekins and top with the bread crumbs. Divide the cheese evenly over the top of the six dishes. Bake for 30 to 35 minutes, or until cauliflower is tender and tops are browned. 6 servings.

Quin-a-Roni

The classic San Francisco side dish is better than ever with the addition of pan-toasted quinoa.

2 tablespoons butter
1 tablespoon extra virgin olive oil
1/4 cup onion, finely diced
1/2 cup orzo or spaghetti broken in small pieces
3/4 cup well-rinsed quinoa
2 1/4 cups chicken or beef stock or broth
salt and freshly ground black pepper to taste

In medium skillet, heat the butter and olive oil until the butter is melted and add the onion. Sauté until the onion is translucent and add the orzo or spaghetti. Stir constantly until the pasta begins to turn golden. Add the quinoa and stir until it is coated with the butter mixture.

Pour in the stock or broth. Reduce heat and cover. Simmer for about 20 minutes and remove lid. Continue simmering until the liquid is absorbed and both the pasta and quinoa are tender. Season with salt and pepper. 4 servings.

Quinoa with Spring Peas and Shallots

Simple and satisfying, this dish is especially good made with fresh shelled peas—but frozen peas will do in a pinch.

2 cups water
1 cup uncooked quinoa, rinsed and drained
1 tablespoon butter
3 small shallots, chopped
1 1/2 cups fresh peas, steamed (or substitute cooked frozen peas)
1/2 teaspoon salt
1/4 teaspoon pepper

In a large saucepan, bring water to a boil. Add quinoa. Reduce heat; cover and simmer for 15-20 minutes or until water is absorbed. Remove from the heat; fluff with a fork.

Meanwhile, heat the butter in a large skillet and sauté the shallots until tender. Add the peas, cooked quinoa, salt and pepper and continue cooking until heated through. 6 servings.

Cheesy Broccoli and Quinoa

Kid-friendly and so easy to make!

2 1/4 cups chicken stock or broth
1 cup uncooked quinoa, rinsed and drained
1/2 teaspoon salt
2 cups chopped fresh broccoli
1 cup shredded Cheddar cheese
salt and freshly ground black pepper to taste

In a large saucepan over medium-high heat, bring
the stock or broth to a boil. Stir in the quinoa and
salt. Reduce the heat; cover and simmer for 15
minutes.

Add the broccoli, stir and continue cooking for 5
to 6 minutes, or until broccoli is tender and most
of the broth has been absorbed. Add the cheese
and stir until melted. Season to taste with salt
and pepper. 4 servings.

Easy Spanish-Style Quinoa

We like this easy side dish as an accompaniment for Mexican food like fajitas and tacos, and it can also be a light main course.

1 tablespoon olive oil
1/4 cup chopped onion
1 cup uncooked quinoa, rinsed and drained
2 cups chicken stock or broth
1 cup salsa
salt and pepper to taste

Heat the oil in a large, heavy skillet over medium heat. Stir in the onion and cook until tender, about 5 minutes. Add the quinoa, chicken broth or broth and salsa. Reduce heat, cover and simmer about 20 minutes, or until liquid has been absorbed. Season with salt and pepper. 6 servings.

Summer Squash Quinoa Casserole

This Southern-style casserole is my family's favorite way to eat yellow squash, and quinoa is the perfect compliment.

4 cups sliced yellow (summer) squash
1/2 cup chopped onion
1/4 cup water
1 cup cooked quinoa
24 buttery round crackers, crushed
1 cup shredded Cheddar cheese
2 eggs, beaten
3/4 cup milk
4 tablespoons melted butter
1/2 teaspoon salt
1/4 teaspoon freshly ground black pepper
2 tablespoons butter

Preheat oven to 400 degrees F and grease a 9- by 13-inch baking dish. In a large skillet over medium heat, cook the squash, onion and water, covered, until squash is tender, about 5 minutes. Drain, add quinoa, and transfer to a large bowl.

In a medium bowl, mix together the cracker crumbs and cheese. Stir half of the mixture into the squash and onions, reserving the rest.

In a small bowl, mix together eggs, milk, melted butter, salt and pepper; add to the quinoa-squash mixture. Spread into the baking dish, sprinkle with remaining cracker mixture, and dot with the remaining 2 tablespoons butter. Bake for 25 minutes, or until lightly browned. 6 servings.

Easy Cheesy Quinoa

Pure comfort food, this simple casserole with a crunchy topping highlights quinoa's delicious flavor.

2 teaspoons olive oil
1 medium leek, white and pale green parts halved and thinly sliced
1 1/2 cups uncooked quinoa, rinsed and drained
2 cloves garlic, minced
3 cups chicken or vegetable stock or broth
1/2 teaspoon salt
2 large eggs
1 cup milk
1 1/2 cups grated Cheddar cheese
2 tablespoons butter
1 cup panko crumbs

Preheat oven to 350 degrees F and lightly grease a 9- by 13-inch baking dish.

Heat the olive oil in a medium saucepan over medium-high heat. Add the leek; cover and cook until tender, about 5 minutes. Stir in the quinoa and garlic, and cook, uncovered, 3 to 4 minutes until the garlic is fragrant.

Add the stock and salt and reduce the heat to medium-low. Cover and simmer for 15 to 20 minutes, or until the quinoa is tender and most of the liquid has been absorbed. Remove from heat and cool for 5 minutes.

In a large bowl, whisk together the eggs and milk. Add the quinoa mixture and cheese and stir until combined. Pour into the prepared baking dish.

In a small skillet, melt the butter over medium heat. Add the panko crumbs and stir to coat crumbs. Sprinkle evenly over quinoa mixture. Bake for 25 to 30 minutes, or until hot, bubbly and lightly browned around the edges. 8 servings.

Quinoa Pilaf

Toasted almonds add flavor and crunch to tender quinoa.

1 1/3 cups chicken stock or broth, divided
1 small shallot, minced
1 garlic clove, minced
2/3 cup uncooked quinoa, rinsed and drained
1/4 teaspoon salt
1/4 teaspoon freshly ground black pepper
1/4 cup slivered blanched almonds, toasted

Preheat the oven to 350 degrees F and grease a 9-inch casserole dish.

In a small skillet, combine 1/3 cup of the stock with the shallot and garlic and cook over medium heat for 2 minutes. Add the remaining stock, quinoa, salt and pepper, and bring to a simmer.

Transfer the mixture to the prepared dish, cover and bake for about 20 minutes, or until the quinoa is tender. Remove the pilaf from the oven and keep covered. Stir in the toasted almonds just before serving. 4 servings.

Quinoa Summer Succotash

Colorful and delicious, this Southern favorite gets a modern update with the addition of tender quinoa and edamame replacing the traditional lima beans.

3/4 cup uncooked quinoa, rinsed and drained
1 1/2 cups chicken or vegetable stock or broth
1 tablespoon butter
3-4 ears fresh corn kernels or 2 cups thawed, frozen corn kernels
1 cup frozen edamame beans, thawed
2 medium Roma tomatoes, seeded, chopped
1 teaspoon paprika
1/2 teaspoon salt
1/4 teaspoon freshly ground black pepper
chopped parsley for garnish

Combine the quinoa and stock and heat over medium-high until it boils. Reduce heat; cover and simmer for 15 to 20 minutes, or until stock is absorbed. Remove from the heat; fluff with a fork.

While the quinoa is cooking, melt the butter in a large skillet over medium high heat and cook the corn kernels and edamame beans, stirring occasionally, for about 5 minutes or until tender. Add the cooked quinoa, chopped tomato, paprika, salt and pepper and stir to combine. Continue cooking for 1 to 2 minutes, or until heated through. Garnish with parsley. 6 servings.

Stir-Fried Peppers, Zucchini and Quinoa

This colorful summer dish of red, yellow and green has a dash of Balsamic vinegar for a pop of bright flavor.

1 red bell pepper, sliced in 1/4-inch strips
1 yellow bell pepper, sliced in 1/4-inch strips
1 green bell pepper, sliced in 1/4-inch strips
2 medium zucchini, sliced
1 yellow summer squash, sliced
3 tablespoons olive oil
1/2 teaspoon ground cumin
1 teaspoon paprika
1 teaspoon dried chili flakes (or more or less to suit your taste)
1 1/2 cups cooked quinoa
salt and freshly ground black pepper to taste
1 tablespoon Balsamic vinegar
2 tablespoons chopped parsley

In a large bowl, combine the peppers, zucchini, squash, olive oil, cumin, paprika and chili flakes. Heat a large skillet and add the vegetable mixture. Cook, stirring occasionally, until the peppers just begin to brown. Add the quinoa and continue cooking until peppers are tender. Remove from heat and season with salt and pepper to taste. Sprinkle with the Balsamic vinegar and parsley and stir just until combined. 6 servings. (Note – you can garnish this dish with a sprig of fresh mint as shown in the front cover photo if you like.)

Quinoa with Edamame, Parmesan and Chopped Eggs

This mild, creamy side dish pairs well with grilled chicken, steak, sausages or veggies.

1 cup uncooked quinoa, rinsed and drained
2 cups chicken or vegetable stock
1/2 teaspoon salt
2 cups cooked, shelled edamame
1/3 cup creamy Italian dressing (or more or less to suit your taste)
salt and freshly ground black pepper to taste
2 hard-boiled eggs, peeled and finely chopped
2 tablespoons shredded Parmesan cheese
1 tablespoon finely chopped chives

Heat the quinoa, stock and broth in a large saucepan over medium high heat. Bring to a boil, then cover, reduce heat, and simmer for about 15 minutes, or until quinoa is tender and all of the liquid has been absorbed. Cool, covered for 5 minutes.

In a bowl, mix together the quinoa and edamame and toss with the Italian dressing. Season with salt and pepper. Gently fold in the chopped eggs and Parmesan cheese, and garnish with chopped chives. 4 servings.

Quinoa with Pesto and Tomatoes

Proof that the simplest things are sometimes the best, this easy dish pairs warm quinoa with garden-fresh tomatoes and pesto for an unbeatable combination.

2 cups chicken stock or broth
1 cup quinoa, rinsed and drained
3 tablespoons prepared pesto
1 large ripe tomato, diced
salt and freshly ground black pepper to taste
shredded Parmesan cheese

Bring the chicken broth and quinoa to a boil in a saucepan over medium-high heat. Cover, reduce heat to low, and simmer until the moisture is completely absorbed, about 15 minutes. Remove from heat and stir the pesto into the warm quinoa. Fold in the chopped tomato and season with salt and pepper. Garnish with shredded Parmesan cheese. 4 servings.

Baked Quinoa "Grits" with Cheddar Cheese

If you've been disappointed by plain-tasting grits in the past, you'll love this flavorful quinoa version enlivened with garlic and Cheddar cheese.

4 cups water
2 cups uncooked quinoa, rinsed and drained
1 teaspoon salt
2 eggs, beaten
1/4 cup (1/2 stick) unsalted butter
1 1/2 cups grated Cheddar cheese
2 cloves garlic, crushed

Preheat oven to 350 degrees and grease a 2-quart casserole dish. In a large saucepan over medium high heat, bring water, quinoa and salt to a boil. Reduce heat to a simmer, cover the pan and cook for about 20 minutes or until quinoa is tender. Remove from the heat and cool for five minutes. Add a spoonful of the warm quinoa to the beaten eggs and then return the mixture back to the pot and stir. Add the melted butter, cheese and garlic and stir. Pour into the casserole dish and bake, uncovered, for 45 minutes or until the top is golden brown. 6 servings.

Quinoa Garlic Polenta Fries

They're a bit of work, but these baked quinoa-polenta "fries" are always a big hit. Golden-brown and crispy on the outside and tender on the inside, they may spoil you for potato french fries forever!

1/2 cup whole milk
1 cup chicken stock
1 tablespoon butter
3/4 cup dry polenta
1 1/2 cups cooked quinoa
2/3 cup Parmesan cheese, divided
salt and freshly ground black pepper to taste
2 tablespoons extra virgin olive oil
1 clove garlic, finely minced
1 cup marinara sauce

Line a standard-sized, rimmed cookie sheet with a piece of parchment paper and set aside. In a large saucepan, combine the milk, chicken stock and butter, and cook over medium-high heat until the mixture comes to a rolling boil. Slowly whisk in the polenta, stirring constantly to combine. Turn the heat down to medium-low, and continue cooking and stirring until the polenta pulls away from edge of pan.

Remove from the heat, put a lid on the pan and cool for five minutes. Add the cooked quinoa and half of the Parmesan cheese and to the mixture, and season with salt and pepper to taste. Spread evenly in the parchment-lined cookie sheet, cover with plastic wrap and refrigerate until cold.

Remove the pan from the refrigerator, cover it with a large cutting board and flip it over. Lift off the pan and remove the parchment paper from the quinoa-polenta mixture. Using a sharp knife, cut into sticks approximately 1/2 inch wide by 3-1/2 inches long.

Preheat the oven to 425 degrees F and line a cookie sheet with a piece of parchment paper. Arrange the polenta fries on top and brush with olive oil, turning to coat. Bake for 45 minutes, turning the fries every 15 minutes to cook evenly, until they are light brown and crispy. While the fries are baking, toss the remaining Parmesan cheese with the minced garlic in a small bowl and reserve.

Remove the fries from the oven when done, and sprinkle them with the Parmesan-garlic mixture, turning to coat. Serve hot with marinara sauce on the side for dipping. 8 servings.

Southern Fried Quinoa and Corn

Make this newfangled old-fashioned dish of corn, quinoa and peppers when summer sweet corn is at its prime.

2 tablespoons olive oil
2 tablespoons butter
1/2 cup chopped green bell pepper
1/2 cup chopped red bell pepper
2 cups cooked quinoa
10 ears fresh corn, shucked, or 4 cups frozen,
    thawed corn kernels
salt and freshly ground black pepper to taste

Heat the oil and butter in a large skillet over medium high heat and add the green and red pepper. Sauté for 3 to 5 minutes, or until peppers are tender. Add the quinoa and corn kernels and cook, stirring occasionally, until corn is tender, about 5 minutes. Season to taste with salt and pepper. 8 servings.

Broccolini Kale Quinoa

Bright green and healthy, this quick stir-fry is also truly delicious.

2 tablespoons olive oil
1/2 cup chopped onion
2 cloves garlic, peeled and minced
1/3 cup chicken or vegetable stock or broth
1 medium head broccolini, cut in 3-inch pieces
1 bunch kale, leaves removed from stems, torn in
  bite-sized pieces
1 1/2 cups cooked quinoa
salt and freshly ground black pepper to taste
1/4 cup grated Parmesan cheese

Heat the olive oil in a medium skillet over medium heat. Sauté the onions until they are lightly browned, about five minutes. Add the garlic and continue cooking for two minutes, until fragrant. Add the broth, broccolini and kale and stir to combine. Cook for 5 to 7 minutes, stirring occasionally, until the broccolini and kale are crisp-tender. Stir in the quinoa and season to taste with salt and pepper. Sprinkle with grated Parmesan cheese and serve. 6 servings.

(Note – for extra color, you can garnish this dish with thinly sliced radishes and microgreens as shown in the front cover photo.)

Quinoa-Stuffed Tomatoes

This light, simple dish is a great way to use an abundance of summer tomatoes.

2 large ripe tomatoes
1 cup cooked quinoa
1 cup panko bread crumbs
1 cup shredded mozzarella cheese
1/2 cup grated Parmesan cheese, divided
2 green onions, finely chopped
2 cloves garlic, minced
1 tablespoon chopped fresh basil
1/2 teaspoon salt
1/4 teaspoon freshly ground black pepper

Preheat oven to 375 degrees F and lightly grease an 8- by 8-inch baking dish.

Slice the tomatoes in half horizontally and scoop out the pulp and seeds. Separate the pulp from the seeds, chop the pulp and reserve. Rest the tomato halves upside down on a baking sheet lined with a wire rack to extract juices, about 15 minutes.

Meanwhile, in a medium bowl, mix together the reserved chopped tomato pulp, quinoa, bread crumbs, mozzarella, half of the Parmesan cheese, green onions, garlic, basil, salt and pepper. Stuff tomatoes with the filling, sprinkle with the remaining Parmesan cheese, and arrange in the prepared baking dish. Bake until tomatoes are cooked through and tops are golden brown, about 25 to 30 minutes. 4 servings.

DESSERTS & SWEETS

Flourless Chocolate Quinoa Cakes

Black quinoa is the secret ingredient that makes these miniature chocolate cakes so rich and delicious.

1/3 cup milk
4 eggs
1 teaspoon vanilla
2 cups cooked black quinoa
1/2 cup butter (1 stick), melted and cooled
1/4 cup vegetable oil
3/4 cup sugar
3/4 cup unsweetened cocoa powder
1 1/2 teaspoons baking powder
1/2 teaspoon baking soda
1/2 teaspoon cinnamon
1/4 teaspoon salt
powdered sugar

Preheat oven to 350 degrees F and grease a muffin tin. Combine milk, eggs and vanilla in a food processor or blender and pulse to combine. Add cooked quinoa, butter and oil and blend until smooth.

Whisk together sugar, cocoa, baking powder, baking soda, cinnamon and salt in a large bowl. Add the quinoa mixture to bowl and mix until everything is moist. Divide batter among 12 prepared muffin cups and bake for 22 minutes, or until a tester comes out clean. Cool before unmolding, and sprinkle with powdered sugar. 12 servings.

Quinoa Strawberry Rhubarb Crisp

Quinoa adds crunch and flavor to an old-fashioned summer dessert crisp.

2 cups warm water
1/2 cup uncooked quinoa, rinsed and drained
4 cups fresh strawberries, hulled and halved
4 cups fresh rhubarb, diced
1 1/4 cups sugar, divided
1 tablespoon cornstarch
1/2 cup apple juice
1 cup flour
1/2 cup dark brown sugar, lightly packed
1/2 cup quick-cooking oatmeal
1/2 teaspoon salt
3/4 cup (1 1/2 sticks) cold butter, diced

Preheat the oven to 350 degrees F and grease a 9-by 13-inch baking dish. In a small bowl, pour the water over the quinoa and reserve.

In a large bowl, combine the strawberries, rhubarb and 3/4 cup of the sugar. In a small bowl, combine the cornstarch and apple juice and stir. Drizzle the mixture over the fruit, stir to combine and pour into the prepared baking dish.

Drain the quinoa and transfer to a medium bowl. Add the flour, the remaining 1/2 cup sugar, brown sugar, quinoa, oatmeal and salt. Add the butter and mix with your hands until the mixture is moist and crumbly. Sprinkle the topping evenly over the fruit and bake for 1 hour, until the fruit is bubbling and the topping is golden brown. Serve warm with ice cream. 12 servings.

Dried Cherry, Almond and Quinoa Cookies

These rich drop cookies studded with almonds and dried cherries are perfect for the holidays.

1 1/2 cups flour
1 teaspoon salt
1/2 teaspoon baking powder
1/2 teaspoon baking soda
1/2 cup (1 stick) unsalted butter, softened
1/4 cup sugar
1/4 cup dark brown sugar, packed
1/4 cup honey
2 eggs
1 teaspoon vanilla
1/2 teaspoon almond extract
1 cup cooked quinoa, cooled
1 cup old-fashioned rolled oats
1 cup dried cherries
1/2 cup slivered almonds

Preheat oven to 375 degrees F and line a baking sheet with parchment paper. In a medium bowl, whisk together flour, salt, baking powder and baking soda.

Using an electric mixer, beat butter, sugar, brown sugar and honey in a large bowl until light and fluffy, about 3 minutes. Add eggs, vanilla and almond extract; beat until pale and fluffy, about 2 minutes.

Beat in the flour mixture, 1/2 cup at a time. Stir in quinoa, oats, dried cherries and almonds.

Scoop heaping tablespoons of dough and shape into balls; arrange on the baking sheet, spaced 1 inch apart.

Bake until cookies are lightly browned, about 12 to 15 minutes. Remove from oven and cool for five minutes before removing cookies from parchment and cooling on a wire rack. About 24 cookies.

Peanut Butter Toffee Quinoa Cookies

With just six ingredients, these easy one-bowl treats combine a slightly chewy peanut butter cookie with chopped chocolate toffee candy bars.

1 cup creamy or crunchy peanut butter
1 cup cooked, cooled quinoa
1 cup brown sugar
1 egg
1/2 cup flour
1/2 cup chopped chocolate-covered toffee bars

Preheat oven to 350 degrees F and grease a baking sheet.

In a medium bowl, combine all the ingredients. Scoop the dough in rounded tablespoons and arrange on the prepared baking sheet. Bake for 10 to 14 minutes, or until lightly browned. Cool to room temperature and refrigerate before serving to set the chocolate. 12 to 16 cookies.

Quinoa Cowboy Cookies

Everyone loves these Texas-sized cookies, chock full of toasted oats and quinoa, chocolate chips and coconut.

1 cup uncooked quinoa, rinsed and drained
1 cup rolled oats
1 cup creamy organic peanut butter
2 tablespoon melted butter
1 cup maple syrup
1 teaspoon vanilla
1 teaspoon salt
1 cup shredded sweetened coconut
1 cup mini chocolate chips
1 tablespoon vanilla

Preheat the oven to 350 degrees F and spread the quinoa on a rimmed cookie sheet. Bake for 5 minutes and remove from oven. Sprinkle the oats over the quinoa and bake for 5 minutes. Remove from the oven and cool to room temperature. Lower the oven temperature to 325 degrees F and line a cookie sheet with parchment paper.

In a large mixing bowl, combine the peanut butter, melted butter, maple syrup, vanilla and salt. Add the quinoa-oat mixture and stir until combined. Add the coconut and chocolate chips and mix thoroughly. Refrigerate for 15 minutes.

Scoop the dough in rounded tablespoons and arrange on the parchment-lined cookie sheet. Bake for 10 to 12 minutes, or until lightly browned. 36 cookies.

Quinoa Oatmeal Raisin Cookies

These old-fashioned oatmeal cookies have a perfect, chewy texture thanks to the addition of quinoa.

1 1/2 cups flour
1 teaspoon salt
1/2 teaspoon baking powder
1/2 teaspoon baking soda
1/2 cup (1 stick) unsalted butter
1/4 cup sugar
1/4 cup packed brown sugar
1/4 cup honey
2 large eggs
1 teaspoon vanilla
1/2 teaspoon almond extract
1 cup cooked quinoa, cooled
1 cup old-fashioned oats
1 cup raisins

Preheat oven to 375 degrees, and line a baking sheet with parchment paper.

In a medium bowl, whisk together the flour, salt, baking powder and baking soda. In a large mixing bowl, beat together the butter, sugar, brown sugar and honey with an electric mixer until light and fluffy, about 3 minutes. Add the eggs, vanilla and almond extract and beat another 2 minutes. Add flour mixture and mix just until combined. Stir in quinoa, oats and raisins and mix until combined, using your hands, if necessary.

Scoop heaping tablespoons of dough and roll into balls; arrange on the baking sheet, spaced 1 1/2 inches apart.

Bake until cookies are lightly browned, about 12 to 15 minutes. Remove from oven and cool for five minutes before removing cookies from parchment and cooling on a wire rack. Makes about 2 dozen cookies.

Raspberry Quinoa Streusel Bars

Red quinoa adds crunch and nutty flavor to these delectable cookie bars, made with both fresh raspberries and raspberry jam.

For the crust:
2 1/2 cups flour
2/3 cup sugar
1/2 teaspoon salt
2 sticks butter, softened and cut in 1-inch pieces

For the streusel topping:
1/4 cup packed brown sugar
1/2 cup rolled oats
1/2 cup uncooked red quinoa, rinsed and
  drained
2 tablespoons cold butter

For the raspberry filling:
3/4 cup raspberry jam
3/4 cup fresh raspberries or defrosted frozen
  raspberries
2 teaspoons fresh lemon juice
1 tablespoon sugar

Preheat oven to 375 degrees F and grease a 9- by 13-inch baking dish

In a large bowl, combine the flour, sugar, and salt. Using an electric mixer on a low speed, blend the mixture and add the softened butter one piece at a time until it is incorporated and crumbly.

Measure out 1 1/2 cups of the flour mixture into a medium bowl and reserve. Distribute the remaining flour mixture into the bottom of the prepared baking pan. Press the mixture firmly into an even layer to form the bottom crust. Bake for 14 to 18 minutes, until the edges begin to brown.

To make the streusel topping, combine the reserved crust mixture with the brown sugar, oats, and quinoa in a medium bowl. Cut the cold butter in small pieces and work it into the crust mixture with your fingers until it is fully incorporated and mixture is crumbly.

In a small bowl, combine the raspberry jam, raspberries, lemon juice and sugar. Mash with fork until combined.

Remove the crust from the oven and spread the raspberry filling evenly over it. Sprinkle the streusel topping evenly over the filling. Return the pan to the oven and continue baking for 20 to 25 minutes, or until the streusel topping is golden brown and the filling is hot and bubbling. Cool and cut in squares. About 24 bars.

SOURCES

These U.S. growers and suppliers sell and ship organic quinoa:

Alter Eco
2325 Third Street, Suite 324
San Francisco, CA 94107
AlterEcoFoods.com
415-701-1212

Bob's Red Mill
13521 S.E. Pheasant Court
Milwaukie, OR 97222
BobsRedMill.com
800-349-2173
503-654-3215

Eden Organic
Eden Foods, Inc.
701 Tecumseh Road
Clinton, MI 49236
EdenFoods.com/store/
888 424-3336
517-456-7424

Edison Grainery
7307 Edgewater Drive
Suite 100
Oakland, CA 94621
EdisonGrainery.com
510-382-0202

La Yapa Organic
194 Orange Street
Oakland, CA 94610
LaYapaOrganic.com
914-220-1740

Pleasant Hill Grain
210 South 1st Street
P.O. Box 7
Hampton, NE 68843
PleasantHillGrain.com
800-321-1073
402-725-3835

Purcell Mountain Farms
393 Firehouse Road
Moyie Springs, ID 83845
PurcellMountainFarms.com
208-267-0627

SunOrganic Farm
411 S. Las Posas Road
San Marcos, CA 92078
SunOrganicFarm.com
888-269-9888

White Mountain Farm
8890 Lane 4 North
Mosca, CO 81146
WhiteMountainFarm.com
800-364-3019
719-378-2436

INDEX OF RECIPES

Appetizers

Breakfasts & Breads

Desserts & Sweets

Dried Cherry, Almond and Quinoa Cookies, 138
Flourless Chocolate Quinoa Cakes, 136
Peanut Butter Toffee Quinoa Cookies, 140
Quinoa Cowboy Cookies, 141
Quinoa Oatmeal Raisin Cookies, 142
Quinoa Strawberry Rhubarb Crisp, 137
Raspberry Quinoa Streusel Bars, 144

Dinners

Asian Ginger Quinoa with Snow Peas, 99
Asparagus with Quinoa, Pancetta and Leeks, 107
Bacon Quinoa, 114
BBQ Chicken Quinoa and Corn, 95
Coconut Quinoa with Shrimp and Ginger, 102
Creamy Quinoa Polenta with Marinara
    Sauce, 110
Crispy Quinoa Chicken Tacos with Avocado, 98
Hearty Quinoa Meatballs in Marinara Sauce, 86
Jerk Chicken with Caribbean Quinoa, 104
Layered Quinoa Cheese Enchilada Bake, 112
Quinoa Bacon Broccoli Bake, 90
Quinoa Burrito Bowls, 96
Quinoa con Pollo (Quinoa and Chicken), 92
Quinoa Crab Cakes, 106
Quinoa Pork "Fried Rice," 94
Quinoa Ranch Casserole, 88
Quinoa, Black Bean and Green Chile
    Enchiladas, 89
Toasted Quinoa Pilaf with Scallops and Sugar
    Snap Peas, 108
Wild Salmon with Quinoa and Green Beans, 100

Salads

Best Quinoa Cole Slaw, 76
Black Bean, Corn, Quinoa and Avocado Salad, 70
Creamy Red Potato and Quinoa Salad, 80
Crunchy Quinoa Veggie Salad with Minted
    Pesto, 77
Crunchy Thai Quinoa Salad with Peanut Ginger
    Dressing, 63
Four Bean Quinoa Salad, 84
Greek Quinoa Salad, 71
Lemon Quinoa Salad with Crisp Vegetables, 66
Quinoa Autumn Salad with Apples, Red Pear,
    Dried Cherries and Toasted Pecans, 72
Quinoa Chopped Salad, 78
Quinoa Green Bean Salad with Crispy
    Shallots, 68
Quinoa Salad with Edamame, Green Beans and
    Cherry Tomatoes, 73
Quinoa Salad with Orange, Avocado and Toasted
    Pistachios, 62
Quinoa Spinach Salad with Orange Dressing, 65
Quinoa Taco Salad with Lime-Cilantro
    Dressing, 82
Quinoa with Summer Tomatoes, Corn and
    Basil, 64
Shrimp Quinoa Salad with Lemon Dressing, 74
Tuna Salad with Quinoa, Tomatoes, Avocado and
    Basil, 81

Side Dishes

Baked French Onion Quinoa and
    Cauliflower, 116
Baked Quinoa "Grits" with Cheddar Cheese, 129

Broccolini Kale Quinoa, 133
Cheesy Broccoli and Quinoa, 119
Easy Cheesy Quinoa, 122
Easy Spanish-Style Quinoa, 120
Quin-a-Roni, 117
Quinoa Garlic Polenta Fries, 130
Quinoa Pilaf, 124
Quinoa Summer Succotash, 125
Quinoa with Edamame, Parmesan and Chopped
  Eggs, 127
Quinoa with Pesto and Tomatoes, 128
Quinoa with Spring Peas and Shallots, 118
Quinoa-Stuffed Tomatoes, 134
Southern Fried Quinoa and Corn, 132
Stir-Fried Peppers, Zucchini and Quinoa, 126
Summer Squash Quinoa Casserole, 121

Soups, Chowders & Stews

Autumn Cheddar Quinoa Soup, 53
Chicken and Quinoa Soup, 44
Cream of Chicken and Quinoa Soup, 52
Cream of Tomato Soup with Crispy Quinoa, 48
Creamy Carrot Soup with Toasted Quinoa, 46
Creamy Mushroom Quinoa Soup, 59
Hearty Beef Quinoa Stew, 60
Italian Minestrone, 50
Lentil Quinoa Soup, 56
Quinoa Corn Chowder, 57
Turkey Quinoa Tamale Soup, 45
Tuscan Tomato, Quinoa and White Bean
  Soup, 54
Vegetable Quinoa Soup, 58
White Quinoa Chili, 47

ABOUT THE AUTHOR

Eliza Cross is the author of six books, including the bestselling *101 Things To Do With Bacon* (Gibbs Smith). Her articles have appeared in *Sunset, Parents, Mountain Living, Western Art & Architecture* and *Mother Earth Living.* She blogs about simplicity, sustainability, good food, organic gardening and personal finance at HappySimpleLiving.com and is the founder of the bacon enthusiast society BENSA. Eliza lives in Centennial, Colorado with her family.

www.ElizaCross.com

Made in the USA
San Bernardino, CA
07 April 2016